SIGNED /

CW00471220

A Formula for Night
New and Selected Poems

In memory of Lauretta Yoseloff, 1928–2013

A Formula for Night
New and Selected Poems

Tamar Yoseloff (signature)

Tamar Yoseloff

To Crysse

with all best ...

April 2016

Seren is the book imprint of
Poetry Wales Press Ltd.
57 Nolton Street, Bridgend, Wales, CF31 3AE
www.serenbooks.com
facebook.com/SerenBooks
twitter@SerenBooks

The right of Tamar Yoseloff to be identified as
the author of this work has been asserted in accordance
with the Copyright, Designs and Patents Act, 1988.

© Tamar Yoseloff 2015

ISBN: 978-1-78172-268-8
e-book: 978-1-78172-275-6
Kindle: 978-1-78172-282-4

A CIP record for this title is available from the British Library.

All rights reserved. No part of this publication may be reproduced,
stored in a retrieval system, or transmitted at any time or by any means,
electronic, mechanical, photocopying, recording or otherwise without
the prior permission of the copyright holder.

The publisher acknowledges the financial assistance of the Welsh Books Council.

Cover:
Cerith Wyn Evans, *Column (Assemblages) IX* (2010)
mixed media, dimensions variable
© Cerith Wyn Evans, photo Todd-White Art Photography, courtesy White Cube

Typeset in Bembo and printed by Bell & Bain Ltd, Glasgow.

Author's website: www.tamaryoseloff.com

Contents

from *Sweetheart* (1998)

Selfridges

My mother held a wire basket in one hand,
my hand in the other. Occasionally she'd pause
to cross an item from her list as she plucked it
from the shelf. For a brief moment she released
her grip and I must have wandered off,
realised I was lost near the butcher's counter.
The full odour of fresh meat, blood and sawdust
hit me suddenly; I looked up to see hares, headless,
strung from metal hooks. I don't think I'd even seen
a hare alive. The butcher was hacking a flank into steaks,
the first cut opening the bright pink of the leg,
the second negotiating bone. But what stopped me
in my tracks was the offal, displayed lovingly on a bed
of lettuce and ice – lambs' kidneys, calves' livers,
sweetbreads, hearts – all the vitals without function.
Just then I felt my mother yank me by the wrist;
she must have scolded me for drifting away
in a strange store, a foreign country. I can't recall.
Twenty-five years later I can still see
those visceral hunks, served up like a delicacy,
indelicate, hearty, more real laid out there
than anything that beat inside me.

In the Chelsea Physic Garden

To tell the truth, it's the names and not
the plants that get you; you thrill to Latin,
the *icus* and *atum*, the beauty of endings.
I like the juicy berries of the belladonna,
the shoo-fly with its little maracas, all
the strange and unloved weeds. Growing up,
the lullabies my mother sang were about
lost love and how sad the past could be, later.
No Rock a Bye, Baby, just the facts.

Now, I love her for it, for the names
she gave me, collections of constellations,
varieties of sea shells, the flowers
we'd pick out walking, bring home to dry.
I used to save abandoned baby birds,
frogs from snakes' jaws. It would always end
in tears. Forgive me, there are things I want
to say, but I have no words, just proper names,
more Latin, prosaic American slang.

In the fairy tale version, we are planted,
not side by side, as you might expect,
but in separate hemispheres, never to meet.
You, the cool fern, adaptable to rainy climates,
and rain or shine, reliable. I'm the problem,
spiky, dangerous, the occasional flower,
poison of course. But exotic. Experts travel
miles to meet me. I dream of leaves, your
soft caress. I guess I'd slash you to bits.

The Butcher Cover

Stu Rosenberg was five foot two without
his Cuban heels. He'd met 'John' and 'Paul'
at the local synagogue. Their 'Ringo'
was an Irish kid, dyed his red hair jet black,
wore gold rings he'd bought cheap on Canal Street.

They played the convention circuit in Jersey,
most of the girls old enough to remember Wings,
did double bills with Nilsson and Mike McGear.
I heard them at the Meadowlands Hilton, 1982;
if you closed your eyes, Stu could fool you.

He invited me to his room, ordered champagne
for *Harrison in 22*. We talked about the day
Lennon was shot, too young to remember JFK.
Then he showed me his prize, bought for a dollar
at a garage sale in Rahway: a real Butcher Cover.

I remember staring at their picture, younger then
than I am now, in their stained doctor's coats,
surrounded by bleeding chunks of meat,
George's hand spearing the head of a plastic doll
like a trophy. It was supposed to be a joke.

The record bosses issued an apology,
rushed the band to Publicity. Suppliers were told to pulp;
some got lazy, pasted the new photo to the old sleeve.
Stu could see the image underneath, carefully steamed
the 'clean' one off, to uncover the real thing.

I was only sixteen, Stu a year older. He wanted
to take me to Liverpool, wanted me to meet his mother.
I never did either. My copy of *Yesterday And Today*
is torn where I tried to peel off the cover,
just board beneath. I don't listen to it anymore.

The Emergency Broadcast System

Sixth-grade history –
and Mrs Shramko unfurled her huge canvas map,
pulling it over the blackboard
like a shade on a window. The old world,
countries divided by colour: yellow Yugoslavia,
East Germany in brown and West in green,
the red mass of Russia staining the north,
the United States candy pink.

I thought the Cold War would be fought,
by definition, on the tundra, the ice floes
of Scandinavia, some arctic plain.
They could go away to sort things out,
no people, no civilisations to be destroyed.
I could see their tanks leaving tracks
in the perfect snow like B-movie monsters,
angry for something to attack.

America could stop worrying.
Those concrete bunkers still sometimes seen
in suburban backyards could be dismantled.
The voice of doom that came on the radio,
suddenly, in the middle of Casey Kasem or Dr Demento
could retire, never again to announce *this is ONLY a test*,
followed by that piercing signal,
preparing us to meet the end.

Fleet

It flows beneath my feet, its subterranean banks
unseen. I glide blissfully though my day,
all liquid, like a fish. I can't understand
what gives this extra lift to my step, as if I'm floating,
and the cars drifting through Clerkenwell Green
are barges carrying sailors home from sea.

But an undercurrent sinks me at Islington:
I sense the bones of the old prison, the plague-dead
dumped straight from their beds, butchers' scraps
staining the water blood red. The old dark brick shifts,
the city groans in its foundations
and spits me out like a sour grape into the street.

Heart-butt

It is heavy in my hand,
the scent of metal and sweat
so similar to blood. Its bullet
could rip through cartilage and tissue,
shatter bone, no repairing
what it broke. But how elegant
the delicate scrollwork chiselled
into silver, dagmaker's name
carved on the lockplate, place and date:
the provenance of a gentleman.

I imagine he cut a fine figure,
ready to do battle for his land
or for the hand of a woman,
his pistol at full-cock.
But it was never fired: they know
by the wear on the flintlock.
Two hundred years later, his treasure
turned up in a Dundee pawnshop.

Unlike the lemon-butt
or lobe-butt, ramshorn or fishtail,
its pommel is shaped from the very thing
it aims for, drawn like a valentine
over the target, big and red,
ready to receive the hit.

Deer

You bring a flask of coffee, brittle cake
that breaks apart in our fingers.
You come here often, just to watch them
work the frozen earth
for what grass is left, heads bowed.

Here in the dark trees
almost anything is possible:
St Eustace came upon a stag at bay
bearing the image of Christ on the cross
right between his antlers.

In the fading light, you look like someone else.
I imagine the trajectory of our affair,
the dazzling week of all-night sex
fizzling to a telephone call.
Our breath clouds before us, a hesitation.

I could go home before it starts,
to a cup of tea and *Now, Voyager*.
I must learn patience, must wait for love
to transfigure me,
the forest ablaze with its light.

The Visible Man

displays his arteries and veins to me
like a road map. I trace the tangled route
to the heart, encased in plastic, every
piece of him defined, each contour scaled
down to size, a man in miniature.

There among memento mori, black jet
dripping like tears, a buffalo's head, a jungle
of taxidermy, he was still in his original box:
The wonders of the human body revealed!
complete with instructions for assembly,
an introduction to anatomy. I would
take him home, build him from scratch.

It was painstaking work, painting each artery,
hooking him up like a Christmas tree;
as he began to take shape, I could almost
sense the things he lacked: the smooth
skin covering hard muscle, a face made up
of all the faces I have loved, the eyes clear,
untroubled. I wanted to understand

everything: the flow of blood and semen,
the beat of the pulse, why each man
I have known snapped shut eventually
when faced with the prospect of love,
of a woman right in front of him
who wouldn't take no. And so I must be
content with this model of a man, a training kit,

until I understand what makes *me* tick,
until I can open the door to my heart,
the way I can lift his breastplate up,
and watch myself in motion, the same
veins and arteries, the same blood.

The Arnolfini Marriage

The mirror came from a junk shop,
where they called the glass *fisheye*. It reflects
every inch of the room, like those globes in school,
when we peeled off the world like an orange
and Greenland was huge. Since then,
I've had a need to see the whole
picture, the dark corners illuminated.

Like Van Eyck's couple, so secure,
their backs to the mirror, facing the future
hand in hand. We can only believe
they were happy. The artist himself
bears witness, his invention
designed to flatter everything it catches:
more fun house than honest.

★

Mother married me off to a merchant I'd never laid
eyes on until the day, surprised
he'd have me in my state. I wore the green velvet,
high-waisted, to hide my shame.
His Dutch was poor; I have no Italian.

The best artist in town,
hired to paint me in my gown,
took one look at me, grabbed a fold of my dress,
hold this up, like so . . . no one will ever guess.

Fish

We followed his path back and forth,
through the tank, translucent
blue body, little skeleton
swaying slightly with movement,
bones glowing, an X-ray
of himself, like the fossil

on your mantel, a souvenir of Lyme,
where amateur geologists
tap at cliffs with tiny hammers,
waiting to unlock the fish
left behind in rock,
like footprints in wet concrete.

The net scoops him up.
He is emptied into a bag of water.
The girl hands over a tenner,
carries him off like a take-away.
She disappears into a sea
of broken deck chairs, rusted tools.

I would like to leave
a small trace of myself behind,
so that you can feel the groove
in the sheets, see my face
miraculously redefined in the pillow,
once I am no longer with you.

The Pub at the End of the World

has no dress code, no Beers of Distinction,
just the local brew, which smells like mildew,
has a head the colour of moth wings.
The walls are a faded yellow, darkened
by nicotine, except around the dart board,
pockmarked by countless failed bullseyes.

There is no jukebox, but a TV
bolted to the ceiling above the bar
is tuned to a documentary on the assassination
of President Kennedy. All three customers
are glued to the car passing the grassy knoll
again and again in slow motion.

You'd have to be lost, cold, badly in need
of a drink, a phone (out of order), but if you
pop in for a pint, the landlord will nod slightly,
watch you from the corner of his eye, wiping
the same glass over and over with an old dishcloth.
You may even feel strangely at home.

There's no last bell. The bar closes
when the final customer gets up to go,
slowly pulls on his coat. A gust of wind
almost pushes him back as he opens the door.
He squints, pauses to make out the pavement,
lifts his collar and braves it.

The Box

opens with the faintest trace of your pomade,
a whiff of coconut. At the top I find a publicity shot
against the stars and stripes: war is over, you are
a young Steinbeck, says the *New York Times*.

Novels flow from you effortlessly. There are more
reviews, all glowing. You are invited to launches,
cocktail parties, gatherings of beautiful men,
all poised to write the next great American story.

About halfway down, the box begins to throw out
disappointments: polite rejection letters, manuscripts
never finished, never read, movie negotiations
shelved. The writing grows uncertain of itself:

women wear the wrong clothes, smoke cigarettes
whose brand names have faded to nostalgia.
I find pictures of your lover on the beach,
like a young Kirk Douglas. By now you are forty;

you teach English to Spanish boys who will graduate
to factories. Their cards are carefully written, thank you
for your patience. Your school in Iowa invites you
to speak to students contemplating a career in writing.

Your face becomes familiar to me in old age,
the established family uncle: unmarried, always speaking
in a child's lilt, preferring us to adults. All traces
of your lover disappear; he remains on the beach forever.

The box is almost empty. A nephew will take this drawing,
the resemblance unmistakable. An old friend will claim
the Stork Club ashtray. I will keep the picture
of the stars and stripes. I never knew you like this:

that first flush of success, that double-breasted suit.

The war has ended, the city is experiencing a boom,
and you are about to open a box of shiny hardbacks,
spines perfect, your name emblazoned on the jacket.

Stragola

A Transylvanian word meaning 'an unfulfilled soul'. Local Romanian
legend says that stragoli can return to cause trouble for the living.

At first you couldn't explain the sensation
as my tongue coaxed hairs at the back of your neck,
the chill that crept up the base of your spine
to the nape, as my nails dragged along each vertebra
like a xylophone. But these are merely party tricks.
I will make myself at home inside your every orifice,
change the flow of your blood like a river off-course,
send your body careening at the precipice,
pound a new beat on your frightened heart.
I will roll out my new-found arts one by one –
such skills can only be mastered if you leave the earth
broken by regret, if you spiral into the underworld
head first. You know I did. Now I am dead, you will
relive every minute we were together, every word
you never said. You will feel it now, like the weight
of a coffin lid over your lovely face. I will plant you
here beside my grave, like a weed stuck fast by its roots,
you will lace yourself to my bones for good.

Barrowland

I have all the time in the world
to play our story once again,
like the songs we knew by heart:
the way you whispered to me
on the dancefloor, light touch
of your breath in my hair,
arms stiff, holding us slightly
apart. You were formal, polite,

not like the boy the week before
who'd tried to lead me outside, pleading
cool air, just to slip a hand beneath
my cotton blouse, hook a thumb
under my bra. I'd pushed him away
and left. How I wish I'd let him
take me home, climb beside me
in my narrow bed. It could have been

my secret. But you cancelled out
all the others that night. I felt safe
in the back seat of the taxi, all warm
and happy, first time in days;
I imagined my mother asleep in her chair,
a single light blazing through the nets.
Next day she'd still be there, sharing
my photo with the inspector

over a cup of tea. They found me
soon enough, my favourite dress
torn wide, blood caked at the lace trim.
I might have wondered why you quoted
Jeremiah like the minister at church,
why you said the Barrowland was sinful
when you went there every week –
eccentric, I figured, a bit shy.

Now I assemble each bit of your face
to match the Identikit, the freckles
dotting your hairline, light hair
close cropped, lips thin, drawn tight
(I feel them brush one last time on my cheek),
squarish chin, clear blue eyes;
I could see a flash of anger harden them
the moment before I died.

It's easy now to say I must have known.
My plot has a view over the city,
a marker stone, an angel pointing to heaven.
In the distance Castlemilk gives way
to the hills beyond. I'd be my mother's age,
keeper of her brown-edged albums,
clippings she'd saved when I was still news,
when I was always beside you.

Ticonderoga

A box of one dozen extra-hard Marvelead
Dixon Ticonderogas, with Ethan Allen,
Hero of 1775, poised for battle on the front.
When opened, they stood to attention, precise
yellow and green stripes capped with erasers.
The sharpener was bolted to the edge
of the desk, ready to receive its recruits.
As I cranked the handle, the pencil became
itself, I could smell the rich lead, the shavings
of its labour, making a point just for me.
A fresh sheet of paper, straight blue lines
guiding my careful letters slowly over the page.

Each morning we would stand beside our desks,
place our hands over our hearts and recite
the Pledge of Allegiance. I could repeat the words,
but didn't understand *republic* or *indivisible*.
Our teacher wore green trousers, a polyester top
with yellow flowers, and a pendant that said
Another Mother for Peace. It was the year
the National Guard were called to Kent State,
a war raged in a country far away. Chalk dust
coated the linoleum, our drawings of mommys
and daddys, houses with chimneys puffing clouds
into a bright blue sky, a sun always smiling.

Biology

The first incision was the worst, the way
my scalpel sank into the strange grey flesh,
the stench, the pig's eyes shut tight,
as if he couldn't face the indignity,
his vital organs exposed. Mr Ormanati bent over
my pig, so close I could smell mints on his breath,
trace the mound of his humpback through
his brown polyester jacket. I longed to touch it,
to see inside his refrigerator, where he kept
his insects; *cold, they are easier to dissect.*
Sometimes he left the closet door ajar
and if I craned my neck I could just see
his foetal deer, asleep in its huge glass jar.

Each night I'd drag the textbook to my room,
stare at diagrams of musculature until my mother
said goodnight, then by flashlight I'd find
my dog-eared Havelock Ellis, real life stories
of every kind of fetish: shoe sniffing, grown men
in diapers, animals, paedophiles, necrophilia.
By day I'd study the postman or the butcher
hoping they'd betray some hidden desire,
or the boy in my class who sometimes stared back
when Mr Ormanati touched the curve of the female
reproductive system with his pointer, pronounced
fallopian softly, like the name of a song.

Arrowhead

Judy's dad must have been past sixty by then
but he still ploughed the field each season.
We'd follow his dust, sniffing the fresh earth,
mining what the ground gave up: shiny mica,
sharks' teeth, arrowheads filed to a fine point.
I had a drawer filled with bird skulls, fossils
from the time the land was underwater;
I imagined my house at the bottom of the sea.

We learned the Lenapes were a minor tribe,
the first pacifists. The boys were disappointed,
they'd wanted scalps – it figured even our Indians
would be boring. They wanted facts and battles,
a sense of history riding through them.
Instead we intoned the names of presidents:
Washington, Jefferson, Adams; a litany
of capitals: *Albany, Salt Lake City, Des Moines.*

I tell my stories to invest them with gravity,
now I understand the way each year dovetails
into the next, how memory sharpens a single day:
*the field is reeling where I stand, the damp smell
of earth, the arrowhead big in my little hand.*
I want it now, to squeeze tight until the tip stabs
the skin. I want to send it flying, so it may show me
what I've missed, piercing the heart of everything.

from *Barnard's Star* (2004)

Barnard's Star

The angels dancing on a pin's head,
the UFO glittering in the night,
the aura left after you have gone –
all of them in my mind.

That faint red dwarf that passes
overhead when I am boiling a kettle
or making the bed
is invisible to the naked eye,

a ball of hydrogen and helium
making for the sun
over eighty miles a second,
certain of its course,

but I know it's there, just as I steer
through a darkened room
by trust, its familiar contours
charted on my fingers.

The Aurora Borealis at Rørvik

The men who live here laugh at us,
they've seen the lights a thousand times.
We huddle in blankets, find
the Plough, the Pole Star – the Pole
seems almost within reach.

At first the light is faint, a stain
on the night. It pulses, brightens,
not quite grey, not green,
invisible in day, like the glowing ghost
that haunted my first room.

They say you can hear it –
the dock's silent, except for the whirr
of winches, salutations of men
spilling from the harbour bar,
so we score it – horns, a trumpet burst.

We have a book with charts,
electrons, protons, molecules
of gas, solar winds – the men here believe
the legend of the swan, caught
between this world and the next.

The men are going home
to goosedown, fireglow, wives.
We can just make out a slender neck,
wings beating a plea to the gods
to bring him back to earth.

Radio Luxembourg

The night he died they played nothing else:
the foreign DJ, a sea of white noise
fading to *Don't Be Cruel* or *I Can't Help
Falling in Love with You*, a low voice

like a ghost, echoing in the darkened room.
With the radio buried under the sheets,
its dial glowing – my own little moon –
the young Elvis sang me to sleep

each perfect note trembling on his lips.
In dreams he was my King Creole,
girls screaming as he thrust his hips
into history, all those years ago.

Now that night too is history:
I remember the songs from that summer,
The Things We Do For Love, 10cc,
or *I Feel Love*, when I first wondered

how it felt, before I knew the sinking
in the heart, all my passion and fire
burnt out. Now when I hear Elvis, I think
of his death, bloated and old and tired,

and those girls who fainted in his wake
old too, their records packed away.

Astrakhan

The lining was black satin
dotted with needlepoint daisies, her initials.
Wide collar, flared waist,
all the rage, like Jackie or Audrey post-Tiffany's,
long white gloves, little calf bag.

Her bags were wrapped in plastic,
stacked neatly on the shelf,
matching shoes for each in rows beneath.
My foot slid right down to the toe,
my toes crowding into the sharp point until it hurt.

There was a flurry of soft pink feathers,
a swirl of Pucci paisley in Day Glo
blue and green, a long cream gown studded
with gold. Folded neatly, returned to their boxes:
Lord & Taylor, Saks Fifth Avenue, Marshall Field's.

To be unpacked by the staff at St Peter's Thrift,
to be twirled around the floor once more
by a volunteer on her coffee break,
or a lady of indeterminate age
who once wanted this dress so much she ached.

The only thing my mother did not give away
was that coat: custom-made,
lining still good, fur still tight,
as it can only be
on lambs not yet born.

Snow in Maine

Knee-high, no, thigh-high,
the kind that packed thick, defied shovels.
The roads were closed so we walked,
do you remember?

The gentle crunch under our boots,
your biker jacket with *twilights last gleaming*
emblazoned on the back, the town draped
in fairy lights, a scene by Currier and Ives.

Couples in plaid jackets
swayed by us, swigging Coors from long-necked bottles
and singing. It was New Year's Eve.

Everything seemed to stop.
I felt weightless, the snow could pillow me,
your hand was ice inside my own,
your words made clouds in the air.

You hated those neat houses submerged, black ice
that slithered under your feet, feeling that the snow
could bury you alive, like the missing climbers
whose bodies eventually rose from the thaw

as if asleep. You are cloudy from your meds
and when you turn to me, you don't know
who I am. Remember the snow?

We lay on our backs and made angels.
I wanted you to see the shimmering
crystals, the tunnel of jewels —
you saw nothing but white.

Moths

We travel to the light instinctively.
The diner is a beacon, sudden in the road
like a UFO. As we enter we are enveloped in heat,
along with the coffee, the burger straight off the grill,
as if the thick air outside isn't enough. We slide
into a booth, our thighs sticking to vinyl.

Our waitress is older than anyone I have ever seen.
Her bones jut from her face as if her skeleton
is trying to escape, rush into the night. I can see
fields in her eyes, the land before houses and roads,
Indian fires smouldering in the distance.
She takes our order, does not look up once;
a vein in her temple throbs as she grinds
her teeth, scribbles *fries, grilled cheese* on her pad.

The grilled cheese is orange, fluorescent
under the humming blue bulb. It glues my lips shut.
You are talking, dipping fries into a pool of ketchup.
I can almost feel your lashes on my cheek,
the warmth of your breath rising, your fingers dusty
with work, old paint, a shimmer of my skin.

We pay, go back into the night. The car picks up
its tune of old motor and stuck gears where it left off,
the radio zeroes in on a voice, a snatch of song,
clear for a moment then gone. The darkness is complete,
except for the moths, illuminated as they are caught
fluttering towards the headlights. In the morning
you will wipe their powdery remains
off the windscreen, then drive away.

The Delaware and Raritan Canal

My mother walks, her arms swinging wide
beside her. She walks every morning
and every afternoon, rain or shine,
winter and summer. I am trying
to keep pace but she is racing towards
her destination; the long towpath
unrolls beneath us, the horizon
shifting with each step we take, the sky
against the gravel, the blue on grey.

A lone sculler slices the water
and as he slides forward, graceful, fast,
the wave he makes ripples the surface
then fades, the water is calm again.
On the opposite shore, an egret
perches on one leg, ready to fish.
My mother is walking so quickly
I am out of breath chasing behind,
so quickly I wonder if she sees

the sculler, the egret, now passing
from our sights. She's into exercise:
at her age (she has read) essential
to strengthen the heart, the bones, even
the soul, although she's never been one
for spiritual contemplation.
When she dies she wants something simple,
no flowers, no ceremony: *just*
scatter my ashes here on this path,

she tells me, *read me a poem or two.*
This is her spot, this canal dug deep
by Irish labourers, with shovels
and bare hands, some hundred years ago.
It flowed across the state, first for trade,
then for pleasure, barges giving way
to sail boats, horses to sunbathers
and dogs, joggers in bright tracksuits,
who heave past, faster than my mother.

But when she hits her stride, she could walk
all the way to the sea, arms sailing
forward, her course certain, past backyards,
playgrounds, great forests of oak and elm,
clapboard churches with neat granite stones
that spell out the local dead, highways
that stretch straight to Maine (their flatbed trucks
holding cargoes we will never know),
the houses of ten thousand people.

The Saints

You see them praying, sometimes headless,
or wearing their hearts, flaming.
Often in groups, cluttering the landscape
with attributes, framed in the glow

of haloed light. They offer gaping wounds
as they float with the angels, silent,
apocryphal. Their benign patrons pose
beside them, tourists in the divine.

They suffer beautifully – Lawrence,
roasted, Ignatius, devoured whole,
Ursula, massacred with her virgins,
Peter Martyr, writing *Credo*

in his last drop of blood. Vermilion,
cardinal, crimson, it sputters on the canvas,
the holy ghost fluttering above –
but their eyes are fixed on you,

the future; you can barely hold their gaze.
A shop girl has the face of Catherine,
she pales as she hands you change,
and the man beside you on the bus,

wise behind his beard, is the Matthew
from your tattered children's Bible,
his lips moving soundlessly – as a siren
parts the traffic, then grows faint.

Studies for a Portrait of a Young Woman, Delft

She knows that she was born
from the descent to Hell,
twisted bodies tumbling
down the Bible's page.

She tiptoes into church, afraid
her heels fall too hard,
takes a pew in darkness,
the pastor starred in prayer.

She shields her eyes
against his glare, white stone
cast as gold, the tiled floor
fretted with light.

Her needle is swift, plants
a garden on plain cotton,
a girl on a swing, flowers
she cannot find in nature.

The men roar in the parlour.
She hears the chink of glass,
breathes their sweat, rich tobacco
from the New World.

She knows how their eyes
trace the lines of her gown,
follow the rise of lace
at the bodice. Their voices fall

when she passes to the courtyard,
takes up her willow broom. It whispers
its small song against the brick.
She raises her face to the sun.

Lekaki

We repeated the name, its 'k's like peaks,
but the old man pointed into the valley; a river
only in flood time, bed like ancient bones.
We began to walk, over stones then boulders;
nothing to them, the men who fled to these caves,
first from Turks then Germans. We hacked
through thorn and gorse, until a wall was in our sights,
then the whole church, as if it had fallen at our feet.

We stood on the threshold, blinded by dark
and the dark gave up its saints, halos flaked
to gold dust, their names spelled out on the wall
as if they'd whispered them, strange words
hanging in airless space, and above, the soldiers
tormenting Christ on the cross, the grinning skull
at the base, and to his left, St George,
a boy, lance raised – his dragon faded away.

Your hand skimmed a crack that severed a saint,
veered straight through the Last Judgement,
bodies tumbling, a cavern within a cavernous Hell,
a slow grind to dust. As we turned to Kardamyli,
the church vanished under vine, once the only house
of God along the Viros, where ferry men had stopped
to pray for six hundred years until the river
seeped away, the last monk arriving on foot.

San Michele

As Tintoretto's towers shrink to toys,
the land receding to lagoon, the island
looming in my sights, I think of monks
who charted maps of a world they'd never see,
their minute graphs and sextants making way
for the dead; a city of graves, divided by church.
I walk between them, brushing leaves away
to read of English girls, travelling alone,
unused to foreign towns, their photos bleached
by weather, eyes that stare from tiny villas
of Carrara marble, slate and polished stone.
They never would have guessed, as they laid out
their Baedekers and gowns, how it would end:
a tethered palace, fever, thunder, rain.

Christmas in London

The skaters glide across the ice like songs
like the skaters who sliced the frozen Thames.

A bus stutters across the bridge; red
lights of OXO, cranes dressed in lights,

the restless Eye lit blue, its tourists lifted
above the skyline, above tower blocks

above the wedding-spire of St Bride's
above the fat dome of St Paul's,

shivering allotments, ragged greens,
the greens where houses stood, where houses stand

no more. The alleys wet with condensation,
darkened streets, the rivers running

just below the ground, the Wandle, the Walbrook,
the Tyburn, the Fleet. The silent churchyards

with their crooked stones, each stone
a marker for a man.

Operation

Every Christmas it was on my list. Maybe
my father, who denied me nothing, actually entered
Toys "R" Us, picked up the bright box, the patient
beaming to show there is no pain, the way
Wile E. Coyote flattens on impact, a halo of stars
circling his head, the Road Runner gloating above,

and my father might have looked at the patient,
organs exposed for each player to remove, gingerly
with tweezers. If you faltered, his nose flashed red,
you lost a turn. I never got one, but I knew kids
who did. In gloomy playrooms among wheeless bikes,
amputee Barbies with wild, matted hair, I was drawn to it.

When my father entered the recovery ward,
I sat by his bed, tattered copies of *Glamor* in my lap.
He looked small, exhausted. Beneath the scar
that extended from collarbone to diaphragm,
his heart was brought blood through a pig's valve,
his breastbone held together by titanium clips

that would trigger metal detectors in airports, even after
he'd removed his coins and keys. I watched his chest
rise and fall, imagined him sliced open, his organs
ticking like clocks, the bands of titanium little jewels.
I wanted to put him back together the way he was
when he was young, a superhero, perfect and whole.

House

The concrete fills the spaces between
the walls and what they held – a child's cry,
an argument, dulled. It hardens, cools.

The house is peeled away like a skin:
a fire protrudes from the shell of a room,
the ghost of a fire gone out.

A mausoleum to newspapers and spoons,
deep-pile carpets, nights consumed
by the bluish glow of the TV,

perched in a field, a grassed-over street
where once other houses stood,
gathering lives together.

The Atlantic at Asbury Park

Palace Amusements has lost an *a*,
another *a*, its *ents*. It seems to say
pale face museum from this distance,
and its chuckling mad boy,
once lit up, has left for good.

I used to watch him twinkle
from Annie's bedroom in the eaves
of her gingerbread house,
once a winter lodging for spinsters.
Her parents were like the elders
in some book. They sat in flowered armchairs
all evening and never spoke.

The wind whipped visitors past the IHoP,
a perched spacecraft, serving pancakes
in sickly syrup. Men basked
in the rain, tattoo ladies peeking
from beneath their sleeves.

Madame Marie hovered over
her crystal ball, the lunar surface
of her face tense in concentration.
Annie and I would sit cross-legged
in the bandstand, making plans.

The carousel house still stands,
its candy-stripe horses flown.
Only the ocean is the same:
black for miles, white caps, grey sky.
At the other end, there's another coastline,
an abandoned arcade, the remnants
of a carousel. I travelled all that way
to see it for myself.

The Nolans in Japan

They paused on the brink of a blinding Tokyo morning:
I could have been dreaming,

thick with sake and jetlag, McTeriyaki,
neon blinking

  Love Hotel . . . Asahi Super Dry

but there they were, their wild red hair streaming,
Rossetti beauties

in tiny Valentino heels, towering
over flunkies

with Yamamoto suits and walkie-talkies.
Then, as suddenly

as they had alighted, they were disappearing
into the choking

traffic mist. I have to tell you everything,
however fleeting:

this city's like a wind-up toy – flashing,
bright – unlike the city

where I live with you, your face beside me
as I am waking.

How could words express this world, reeling
out of reach –

a place you don't exist where I have seen
The Nolans, leaving

in their tinted-window limousine,
faces fracturing,

Japanese teens giggling through their hankies
in disbelief?

Florida

We breathe Copper Tan, roasted cashews, adrift
in a sea of Day Glo – Windex blue, flamingo,
a yellow like the ball of sun that sears my shoulders.

Pale next to musclemen, their perfect girlfriends,
you look out of place. I have brought you here,
it's my fault. You make more sense in rain.

Suddenly a band strikes up, all oompah brass,
kettle drum. Your face is stone. I slide my tongue
over my lips to seal your taste.

Nearby a child drops his perfect sphere
of pistachio on the sidewalk, starts to wail,
his face a carnival mask of pain.

We turn a corner and there's the ocean. A toy boat
bobs on the horizon. We have come to the end
of the country, run out of words.

from *Fetch* (2007)

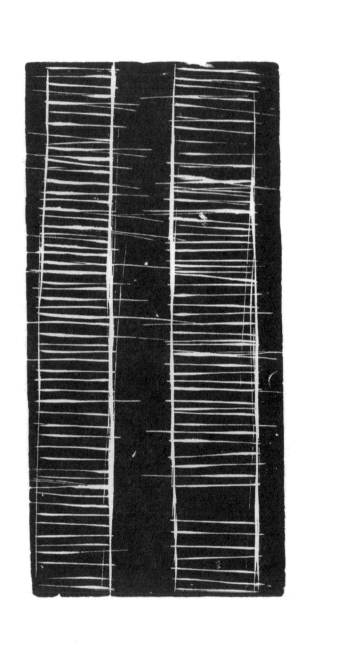

Fetch

*n. 1. A stratagem by which a thing is indirectly brought to pass,
or by which one thing seems intended and another is done; a trick; an artifice.
2. C17: of unknown origin. The apparition or double of a living
person; a wraith.*

1

I send her out
into the cold dark night.
She rides a bus to the edge
of town, enters a bar.

See her hair, nearly black
in the dim room, skin
translucent. She orders a beer,
downs it in one

The men sit with their backs
against the wall, watch her
order another, cross
the floor, take a seat,

while I am safe
at home, wondering if I should
cut my hair – too long, I think
as I catch myself in the mirror.

She smiles at her reflection
in the jukebox, the glare of neon
like a halo, plays with a strand of hair,
chooses *Are You Lonesome Tonight?*

A quarter clinks into the slot,
the mechanical hand lifts
the black disc, slips it in place.
The arm swivels over

needle poised. The men
check out her ass, her legs.
Skirt's too short, I think,
pulling mine over my knees.

2

I choose her uniform –
sunglasses, trenchcoat.
She needs to lose herself
in a crowd, to be invisible.

She enters Main Street
at 2:32pm precisely,
sidewalk slick with rain,
sights him moving south.

Easy to spot in a crowd:
I'd know the arc of his shoulders,
his particular, easy gait,
from a mile away.

She must report
where he goes, who he meets,
if he still wears that blue shirt.
She's made for this,

tails him like a cipher,
a girl he might think
he knows from somewhere,
but can't quite place.

She keeps her distance
like I taught her, hugs the walls,
will duck into a doorway
the exact moment he turns.

He doesn't turn. He is a man
who never looks behind him,
although today, something
stops him in his tracks,

maybe a small prickle
of déjà vu, like a finger
tracing the curve of his spine,
like someone treading on his grave.

3

I am thinking of her
constantly, the way she walks –
someone once told me
I walk on my toes –

the way she holds a pen –
I have a ridge on my finger
where my biro rubs –
the way she writes him down:

He's drinking coffee, his thin lips
grazing the side of the cup,
the contents still hot, his mouth
making little kissing motions.

He smells of cut grass
and tobacco, runs his fingers
through his hair, gazes into
the distance, as if he's seen a ghost.

That was her last report.
Somehow she's managed
to throw me – she's learned
the principles of treachery –

now I wait for them both
to return, counting the hours
like a rosary, the pang
of loss pressed on my ribs.

4

After days, I spy her
in the lobby of a motel,
wearing my brown coat.
She smoothes it over her hips,

determined, steely. I want to
shake her by the shoulders,
the shape of her bones familiar,
but it's too late.

When he sees her, his face
changes completely as if he
has never seen her, as if he
has seen nothing else.

He says *your hair is different*,
and runs his fingers through it,
I can feel the crush of his lips
as he pulls her close by my collar.

In a room on the third floor
she unbuttons his shirt (the blue one),
spreads her hand full
over his chest, his coarse hair

blossoming under my fingers.
She has stopped breathing. He is hard
against her, pushes her legs apart.
I have stopped breathing.

On the wall above the bed,
a faded Monet poster:
a girl in a white hat
adrift in a field of poppies.

As their bodies blur in the tangle
of bedclothes, I feel my skin
go numb; the power to receive
his touch is gone, his face goes dark.

She has found herself without me.
I am stranded in a station
at midnight, where the train rushes
through without stopping.

5

It can only end
one way – on the edge of town
on the darkest night I can imagine,
and she's alone. So alone

she can feel the ache rising
from stomach to heart to brain.
She has lost us both. I knead the vein
on the side of my head, throbbing.

I knock a whisky back,
she feels a burning
in her throat. This is going to be
hard, I think, steering her

away from the safety
of a street lamp, into the unknown.
At the other end of the street,
a car swerves into being

takes the edge off the corner
onto the sidewalk.
She will never know
what hit her.

Black Water

I emerge from sleep, my tongue puddled.
You stand against the door, the light
behind you. You could be clay or iron,
I know your shape –

                    you were in my dream,
how clear you were – I could feel your touch.
We were in a house I haven't seen in years,
a shell – roof blown off, blackened eaves.

Long before you, places existed, objects
that have lost their definition.

I begin to focus. You are at the window.
I follow your gaze and see the clouds
clot on the horizon, a boat trailing its ghost,
the water's flat black surface, like ink or blood

and I think of the cold plunge,
                    water filling my mouth.

I run a bath, watch it curl with steam, then
ease myself in. Red spreads across my skin.

Illumination

Gold leaf, cadmium, ochre, saffron –
indelible once set on vellum.

The monks ground azurite and lapis
for perfect blue, took care

to cleanse their hands of poison
that made words sacred.

We place our fingers against
each other's lips, a vow of silence,

sense the touch mark even after.
I am brimming with words

but none can hold that moment
when our faces, edged in gold

glinted in the water's mirror,
the invisible sun within us –

so I let them fly, lead white
against a white sky.

Shadow

*...how can a man throw his shadow, make this the illumination
of his experience, how put his weight exactly – there?*
                                                    – *Charles Olson*

When we look back it is there, that
darkness of ourselves born
of days when the sun was blinding.

I trace what's left on the pavement
where you walked, schist or shit,
your heavy feet relearning those lost steps,

a dance we moved to once,
a shadow play in liquid streetlight,
late lamps, sodium glow of stars.

What mattered was matter, the precise
weight of you, so many ounces
of flesh and blood,

your hand on my shoulder, solid
and light like music,
our empty glasses on the table,

beakers for what cannot be
contained; the feather
of our lips, our touch.

Gorse

I breathe its scent, like sweat
on skin. The rain has brought it out.
Yellow settles on my scarf, too yellow,
a warning. Its branches shimmer water,
buds tight to bursting. Beyond the green stem,
its lobed leaves, I can see the thorns, daggered
in branches that anchor it to earth.
It owns this place.

I would like to plant
my fingers deep like roots, spread
like a dark stain, vigorous and hearty.
I would like to shed my petals, my silk touch,
before the final sharp prick
that draws blood. I trespass here,
I am only passing through. I close
my eyes and see an afterlight, a shock of yellow.

The Firing

If I had any chance of recovery, this passion would kill me...
I have coals of fire in my breast.

— John Keats

Our bodies, ignited by touch; however light,
flesh can singe with pleasure, the heart
can burn itself to cinder.

We leave relics in the sheets,
our sweat and skin, what's dead of us.
In the half-dark I listen

for the shuttle of my heart.
Blood wells up through a cut
to taste the world.

I am a vessel, open
to your body. If only you could
move through me, enter

the spleen, the coiled intestine.
You are already in
my eye, my brain.

★

Fire takes the manshape
like a lover: the clumsy arsonist,
the heroic father, the monk

in saffron robes. No matter
what they believed,
how they lived, in the end

reduced to this: a ribcage
forged in flame, curving like
the branches of a tree.

★

In the story my mother read me,
the tin soldier burned for love,
reduced to a molten heart,

the dancer's tinsel rose
shrivelled to a dark fist.
I longed for the happy ending.

Strange shapes would form
in darkness as I lay in my bed
at night, wondering

what it was like to die.
I found a bird's skull in the yard,
ran my finger over the beak,

the eyeless hole,
the smooth cranium,
then buried it in the ground.

★

A man stands before a wall
of fire, holding a cross
on a chain against his heart.

His likeness is on ivory
and although so small,
I think I see the flicker

in his eyes as he beholds
the woman who held
this image to her heart

four hundred years ago.
To think of the flame
he burned for her

snuffed out, four hundred
years in his grave, his love
reduced from flesh to bone

to soot; but flesh remains
in memory, the feel of her skin
beneath his fingers, like fine clay.

★

Coal and ironstone, silica, bole,
sea earth, marl, the soil yields
hard treasures, breaks down matter.

In the hilltop cemetery the graves
fall in on themselves,
marble crumbles to dust,

loved ones tumble
into each other's arms, their bones
knit and form a whole.

★

Gold fillings, titanium,
a wedding ring, calcium.
What doesn't burn

is sifted out. A light package
without heavy limbs
and troublesome heart.

When I die, scatter my ash
on water, so I curl the waves
on a cloud of dust,

each particle of me alive
to sunlight, floating,
a little boat of myself.

Tiger

He stalks the wilds of the duvet
in this nil-star hotel room,
just a double bed and a bidet.

On the street, the ladies of the Barbès
saunter in five-inch heels, buy
Medjool dates, long okra fingers,

the men bask in a cloud of Gauloises,
drink sweet coffee that leaves a sludge
in the cup. Two floors up

you sing to me of drunken sailors,
whores straddling the harbour;
your fingers tease guitar strings.

I whisper to you how the foie gras
slipped down my throat,
the Sauternes, silk on my tongue.

Beneath the tiger's eye, your hand
is moving up my thigh. I am all
polished spruce, catgut,

you make me sing. We recreate ourselves
as Cubists, intersect tongues and limbs,
pliant and supple, animal.

Shalott

There was a girl once
who could speak three languages,
who knew plant names and could type.
She had fair hair that fell into her eyes.
Maybe she died. The woman
who lives here now is bone-thin, worn
like this shattered plate. She rages
at the weeping tree, her weary breasts.
She knows about blood, considers
how to summon it, lovely potion –
the razor and its buttery touch,
the cough that brings it up, shining
on a white handkerchief. She craves its
sticky taste; runny honey, spunk.
She wanders the streets, feels
the riverbed swell under her feet.
She sees men watching her, eyes
like questions, remembers their hands
sliding over her as if she were glass.
She can undress them, feel their pricks
growing in her hand, vessels of blood.
At night she hears the blackbird –
lovesick, lightpoisoned – singing his
heart out, the fox crying to no one,
her fur bristling in the cold, and she flies
out of her body to meet them,
her barge balanced over the city
in a bolt of lightning.

The Venetian Mirror

When I first hung it in our bedroom we could not sleep all night,
it was like having the moon for company, so bright it shone.
— Jim Ede

1

Silver has its day, recedes
to reveal the surface beneath

gone black –
its own Dorian moment.

It reflects back what we have
not been able to understand,

an abundance lost, just hinted
in the etched leaves, tendrils lacing

the frame. What's inside is
rust, a pox on a lovely face,

still we trade its dimensions
for our own: dumbstruck, vain.

2

The basilica behind a slick
of rain, gold diminished

to dun. The colour of nothing.
The bulk of it jagged

on the darkening sky.
The end of day, odic light

illuminates a shrivelled rose;
all the sadness we contain

in this drop of rain, its
crystallised gloom.

3

The ghost hulk of the palazzo
leans into the canal. Narcissus crazed.

Tarnished jewels, pink marble
dulled to flesh. Shiver of a ballroom

out of season, sliver of broken
glass, the first glistening of frost,

as the campana strikes,
mourns itself in echo.

The Angle of Error

This is a more complex geometry than I had intended

I have charted this on my graph of unease –

your hand in motion –
        push, twist, splay

the arrowed grass in a rain-soaked field, each blade defined –

        the grey stone of disappointment.

Your face picassos –
        I can no longer picture you whole.

An endless spirograph of a narrow room, an off-season coast –

        my head slanted to catch your mouth
your hand sphering my wrist –

        the gazetteer of hurt.

I think I'm moving forward
        but I'm not

my heart pounding its old song – *stop, stop, stop*

navigating a tiny circle
        a crutch dragged in the dirt.

Silk

Glissando   the small
shimmer of my sashay.
Ssh, or you'll miss me.

        You'll miss me,
the cool dip as I slip
from your fingers:

the one that got away.
A miraculous fish,
all glide and guggle,

as I dive into my sea
of troubles.
                You've only
skimmed the surface.

I wear this, precious gift
of industrious worms,
        so I'm ingrained

in your memory, like
the green light, red room,
the geisha gloom

of black silk   slick
under your fingers
as you undo those

fiddly little buttons
one by one, and open me:

a Pandora's box,
a bag of tricks,

a billet-doux
addressed to someone else.

Portrait of a Couple Looking at a Turner Landscape

They stand, not quite touching,
before a world after storm.

There are drops of moisture in her hair,
in his scarf
             the colour of a gentler sea, his eyes,

while trains depart every minute, steaming
into the future, where the hills

unroll themselves,
vast plains of emerald and gold

        (she undressed for him, slowly,
        her skin like cloud under dark layers)

after rooms of Rubens and Fragonard, flesh dead
against old brocade
             (their flesh alive in the white sheets).

There are trains departing.
                    When they part
it will be night, outside a theatre, near the station,

        and the sky will be blown with stars
too dim to see in the glare of neon.

They will stand on concrete and asphalt,
                    the innocent shining sands

lost. The world tilts to meet her face,
he holds her face close

and something closes in on them,
the weight of silence in the street,

the winter horizon, bright, huge,
the moment before
                    the sky opens and it pours.

The Red Hill

after Elisabeth Vellacott

The midmorning ridge, dreaming
fields. Harvest. A harvest moon
last night, and today, a hare
balanced on the edge, briefly.

Remember this. It may not
come again, the razor sky,
the trees, rust and leaves
in the air. Perfect stillness.

Commit it to yourself
so that it enters your blood,
returns as a heartbeat
the second before you move

forward, and it is shattered.
Your mark will be erased
by wind, hard rain,
by the way you race

from one place to another,
wanting so to lie down,
to fit the earth around you,
taste the ferrous clay.

Remember this, before
it shifts to brick, asphalt,
to a white curtain, a bare room;
many rooms will clutter your head.

Beyond the ridge, the little house,
the fire lit. In it are people
you love. They are waiting.
You close your eyes

and the field breaks into lines,
a sketch of a field, it blurs
and aches, gives way
to white. You fill in the rest.

Voyage

The train sails through fields, docks in middle-
manager cities: Coventry, Milton Keynes,
the track before us a fact of our expansion,
the night inevitable: sick phosphorescence of lights
coming on, of platforms rushing past,
the names of towns indecipherable with speed,
their tower blocks blown back in a sudden squall.
On the page a man is drowning;
I only have to close the book to forget him.
He's history. The present is about the train
hurtling past on the opposite track, steering
for where I've just been; the flotsam of travel:
the paper cup, the empty miniature,
the folded tabloid. Old news. Salt on my tongue.

The Sea at Aberystwyth

This is the end
of the world. The wild west, but not the frontier.

The old monster is roaring on the beach again.
Kids run along the front in shirtsleeves, chasing

his fury, one great dark wave after another.
Oh rain, wash them clean.

The Norwegian tourists bask in a thousand ways
of getting wet. The windows of the Marine Hotel

are caked with guano. Maybe the rain will do
the trick. The seagulls swerve in the air stream.

The Spice of Bengal dims its lights, its one customer
sated. Time to wander into night. What we want

lies broken on the shore, what we can't have
stays black on the horizon;

the moon of the zebra crossing
flashing for no one.

from *Marks* (2007)

If you think of the forms and light of other days, it is without regret
– Samuel Beckett

1

I have marked
      the clock's   black arm
winter movements   of the stars

where you left off speaking
    traces of you   in all things –

the white space where you were
      standing

        all explodes around you
          an invisible halo –

angel of dust   and light

the spiders   understand
   weave intricate maths in the eaves
      hatch   in the artificial heat

while outside
      winter   my winter haunt

I have this in my body
coldness

the ice   breaks
a song   in the trees

fingers of condensation
    drag the windows clean

what I see   I have always seen

you were always
        in front of me
blocking the light

2

Blades of grass through snow –
                                    snow falling

flakes on my tongue
cold kiss

I used to do this
when I was a girl   my mouth
                                    open to the sky

things don't join up now

I track the prints
of some animal   through the white

hieroglyphs
in a field
                    they trail off

          I have followed the wrong lead

my pulse
a little morse of blood

          any more than this
          I can't make out

3

A finger blades a line
straight   from throat to womb

peel back my skin   reveal
          the workhouse   of heart and lung

          blood
slogging   through my veins
          my discontented bones

4

all that inner space   *one never sees*
          the brain and heart
and other caverns   places where marks
          don't show

          not like skin
                    it carries every cut

          those prints flower like a bruise

I turn   turn again
          show my good side   the good side
it's never the same twice

          myself in my skin
          what I understand

all that inner space
          and no way out
                    the bars become a window
through which to see yourself

I will return to
          the scene of my betrayals
          the kindly dark

5

Slice the dark
    my razor   margin of error

no maps —

watermarks
fingerprints
Roman road beneath the field   old earth
    a page
        erased

we unsleuth/ unsheaf
    cut a path with our bare hands

no guides —

reservoir covered over
memory of water
the night
    recovered

trial and error   we find the centre

6

Hold it in your hand
hold it to the light

    bird   bone
        breaker
               stone
delicate crevice of ice –
              broken

    beaker
        hone
      high   held
        blight
throw it to the sea
hold it tight

delicate surface of bone –
        old white

7

Radio waves in air
    break over me

words
   just audible
between broken frequencies

sound   without
   meaning

I mean

the sky darkens to hold
   its weather

to go on and get on
   my only care

what holds us here
   is weather
      whether or not   we are

8

A box of snow
       the moment

I melt away
       an echo   of myself

words are
       light

they hold no ice
       wise   crack

a long white turnpike
       a road   to no –

9

My mark on the page

a smudge

my voice   breaks up
     down the wire

long   distance

we can't bridge this

the margin is

where you set it

open the book   see
     words   as horizontals

cross   word

here's where you draw the line

words at sea   an   s   o   s

10

I will return to
the broken bone
the open page
the house of ice
the radio waves
the wave goodbye
the morse of blood
the winter trees
the frequencies
the clock's black arm
the wounded path
the Roman road
the spider's web
the ocean bed
the weathervane
the chance of rain
the fractured line
the fretted light
the box of snow
the flowered bruise
the empty room
the blades of grass
the razor's gash
the old cold kiss
the body's slog
the touch of skin
the heart the heart
the kindly dark

from *The City with Horns* (2011)

Concrete

There are no lyric dimensions
to its flat grey surface

no freedom in its hardness;
it houses many secrets

in its brutal expanse, provides
solutions. It is not charming

like daffodils or a pink tutu.
It refrains from statement,

turns its back to black words,
angry crows; it fills the bombsite.

It is not vulnerable
like the pale mirror you raise

to your face. You will fling yourself
against it, see what breaks,

Cryptographer

after Quattro Stagioni: Inverno *by Cy Twombly*

I string together little fables
in a language no one understands.

So much wounds me.
I write it down, cross it out:

a formula for contentedness –
instead so much violence.

They could kill me with a look.

You come to me in dreams,
blurred touch of your hand,

your name scrawled on every wall.
Your shadow stalks me.

How we got here I don't know,
there is nowhere else.

Winter obliterates us, dizzy light,
our white youth.

Siberia

They are drinking tea by the samovar
and he is watching the steam
rise from her glass, the way her lips
flutter over its rim.

She takes from his outstretched hand
the tiny creature caught in amber –
the colour of her eyes.

She says, if you listen to the snow
it's like your heart shattering slowly.

Reading *Ulysses* in the Teri Aki Sushi Bar

He would have liked the concentric circles
of the California roll, whorls of salmon and avocado,
brightwhite rice, the ginger fanned
across the plate – like Molly Bloom,
her legs apart – the saki hot
in his throat, a trill of syllables.

He would have admired my discipline,
my quiet journey with Leopold
and tuna maki – squintyeyed
over the page, the words
running away from sense.

The Dublin streets swell with rain,
delicate perfume of dung, and
there's a man hurrying home,
brown eyes saltblue, with no umbrella.
　　　　I will know him, oh yes, by the shrug
of his shoulders, hunch of his coat,
the way he looks up, suddenly,
comprehends

　　　　　　that somewhere a girl, pretty,
captures a fishy gobbet in her chopsticks,
raises it to her lips, that first bite releasing
brine, bladderwrack, the green rot
of the ocean floor.
　　　　　　If only he
could sit across from her, worship
her perfect little teeth.

He will pass me on the street
one evening when the rain
smells like the ocean,

       flame memory for an instant
before we turn our separate corners,
pull our collars to our throats.

Mannequins on 7th Street

for Robert Vas Dias, after Anthony Eyton

We desire them to be perfect:
limbs without blemish, Malibu-bronzed,
robed in fuchsia and gold, smouldering
goddesses in a city leached to grey.

We, merely flesh, race past, hail cabs,
jump buses, never to strike
their timeless pose.

We must embrace the gift of the street,
the glare of chaos, of things being various.
The frail instant needs us to record it;
the mute made audible, still life animated.

They keep watch from their temple
of glass, stranded in silence, all dressed up
and nowhere to go.

The Sadness of the Scrapyard

A phrase used by Margaret Drabble to describe
the work of the artist Prunella Clough

A plastic arm, tiny fingers grasping
nothing. One shoe, the other
long missing. No attachments

in this corrugated space,
this ochre mound of loss
where things shed their colours.

To love the scraggy ends
is to love everything;
our heaven's a slab of ruin,

broken glass and scrap
piercing skin, heralding
rusty blood, cloudy courage.

What is hard we'll soften
with our shapes, what we see
indefinable in the heap

but still something gleams
even when all around us
is asleep.

Blackwork

A type of embroidery which dates from the sixteenth century

A broken heart
Backstitched on a linen sleeve in black;
The dye corroded, like my love, the threads
Which held us worn away. You take your leave.

You take your leave.
I count the weary days in lengths of crewel,
Blossom withers on my bodice, dies.
I spin a gauze in blue, to match your eyes.

To match your eyes
To mine again, I'd give my own; what need
Have I of sight without you in my weave?
In my grief, the rose gives up the ghost.

Give up the ghost,
Devastated soul, and sing your last.
No fairings will he bring to show his love;
A black cockade I'll wear above my heart.

Stamps

Long after the letters they carried have vanished,
they flourish, unstuck from envelopes, edges
like stiffened lace, the watermark, a ghost of order.
There is value in error: the Inverted Airmail,
its kamikaze Curtiss printed upside-down,
the three-cent Farley's Folly, the Swedish Yellow.
They are prized, these rare mistakes.
But you keep even the most common for the sake
of completion. Strange princes, exotic flora,
clipper ships: all cancelled, their journeys finished,
their countries gone from the map, dusty on the tongue,
now news speeds invisibly through secret cables.
What you hoard is the old world in all its slowness
magnified beneath your glass.

London Particular

The ghost of my father
emerges from a doorway at noon on Piccadilly,
his hair just turning grey, like the London day
he's sailing through in his double-breasted suit.

No more than smoke and mirrors –
that's what the city does
with its alleys, its burnished brown wood pubs,
scrappy parks, tower blocks toppled to leave

a legacy of empty lots. Locations
which are lost, which lose me
in their ordinariness, the light caress
of a stranger's arm as I pass by.

These days I find the haze
growing thicker, all the things I can't remember:
names, dates, faces. The city renders everything
anonymous, disposable.
                        It happens too with age:

same age as he was when he first arrived,
war still clinging to these Blitz-rung walls,
piles of rubble and dust, bilious fog
hovering like an illness in the sky.

City Winter

There's nothing more beautiful:
a smudge of taxis and buses
crawls across the empty grey; a muddle
of faces – lovers, long-lost friends –
rises to greet you. The mercury drops,
darkness yields to streetlights, headlights.
The edge of your known world.

What you've missed –
hidden behind the bright dome
of a church, the slashed glass
of an office block, massed clouds.
Last greens of summer
still in your head, a sudden recollection
of heat – *nothing more beautiful*

*than knowing something is going
to be over.* You walk the streets, the map
ingrained in your feet, stare
into uncurtained rooms
lit and ready for intimacies –
you've been outside yourself
too long. What you want

you won't find here. A train
leaves the city, its complicated tracks
weave past buildings still to be built,
girders lifting beyond the horizon,
its passengers bound for those lit rooms
flickering like grubby stars
on the outskirts.

Weather

You ask me how I know before the first fat drops fall from the sky.
When I was nine I broke my wrist and all the kids in my homeroom
signed their names on the plaster cast. When the surgeon sawed it off
they came away too, forgotten now. I stared at the pale arm I'd lost
touch with, like something dredged from the bottom, like the face of
the dead president furred and flickering on the TV screen, like the first
snow witnessed by the grandmother I never met, blinking in the cold
sunlight of a new country. I feel it in the air, in the hairline of my bone
knitted whole again: that ancient thing which will endure without me.

Mud

after Howard Hodgkin

I see the scuffs and knots and bruises:
what a body takes.

The sea at night, tarmac road –
an obliteration, a mistake.

The Japanese master contemplates
the landscape from his mountain –

I clear the mud from my window,
wait for a revelation:

the antiseptic tinge of boredom,
silt of the airless room.

Now it's quiet, the memory
of spring behind us. Nights drawing in,

the tide is out, so when I walk
the edge of the shore my feet stick fast.

What a body needs:
the green warmth, someone to hold.

Lemons

Leaves in shadow, back-
        lit, sun pooled, denied;
                new leaves

purpling to clasp
        their flower, flower
                bulging to fruit,

sour promise —
        pulp smutting
                a frosted glass,

a terrace, acid
        on my tongue;
                the rasp of wasps.

A storm clots
        on the horizon, ants march
                the parched footpath,

warriors, workers;
        rust of old iron,
                of blood.

A cloud muscles
        small drops of rain,
                cold drop

of lemons, puckered
        suns (more like moons), fizzing
                against the stone wall,

the woodpile
        rich with ants,
                heavy air.

We promise ourselves
    a memory of sun,
        buy the postcard.

The lemons are having none
    of it. They bask in their gloom,
        refuse

to be sweet,
    leave the residue
        of their sticky kiss.

Jetty

after Peter Doig

You stand at the end. It is winter.
The water, slivered through bare wood slats –
brackish, dark – sways with the movement
of small disturbances,
                              the life
of the lake, what life there is
this time of year.

You stare into the flat expanse of water;
it does not give you back yourself.

In the middle distance, a canoe drags
its past behind it, the water
clears a path then closes. It leaves no trace.

Canada geese rise in formation –
a compass pulling south, a 'v' for *vagrant* –
their cries like children's laughter
amplified over the surface of the lake

                              and the mountains
shocked into whiteness through a muddle
of cyprus and pine.
                        Everything
dissolving   even as you see it.
The eye takes in
the canoe, already further, further
than you thought it could drift
in the brief moment you looked away,
                  and the mountains further still.

Everyday there is less.

You feel the wood beneath your feet,
hard but pliant, bending slightly with your weight,
water rushing under you, the deepness
of the lake.
          You sense these things
altogether, understand nothing,
your mind drifting to a point beyond,
a nowhere.

You once knew how deep it is, how wide;
forgotten now. You've forgotten the names
of certain plants and birds.
You meant to buy a book, binoculars
to see through the trees,
black fences enclosing you in dusk.

It is winter.
The water would chill you to the bone.
                    There have been lakes,
reedy and lush in summer. There have been oceans,
wide beaches, there have been people you've loved
running along the waves.
                    There will be others.

You have forgotten so much;
the constellations your father taught you as a child.

The cold glow of stars, so far away.

You can't see the opposite shore;
soon it will be too dark to see anything
but you can't turn back.

     Something keeps you here,
entranced by the black lake, little glints
appearing on its surface.

Even this feels too vast, this small corner
of the world closed in on itself by the woods,
the mountains.
     And you are smaller still
as night veils you, makes you invisible,
a distant speck, like the stars; the canoe,
somewhere else, further along,
out of your sight.

The City with Horns

'Every good artist paints what he is.'
— Jackson Pollock

'If Jackson Pollock tore the door off the men's room in the Cedar it was something he just did and was interesting, not an annoyance. You couldn't see into it anyway, and besides there was then a sense of genius.'
— Frank O'Hara

1. *The city with horns*

like the steer he claimed he lassoed out West,
all ten-gallon hat and heft, hugging the bar at the Cedar,

like a bull, great bulk of the Minotaur,
naked and erect, Europa bowing at his feet;

the streets of Europe choked with blood and dust,
as he wakes in a sweat from a dream of death,

horny again, no broad brave enough to fuck him,
this beast of a man, a real artist, no bullshit,

like the sax at the Five Spot or some
Village dive, a diva with skin like coal,

like the angel choir, cabbies leaning on their horns
as he trumpets down the Bowery, just the guy

to wrestle this city to its knees, *exciting
as all hell.*

2. Lee Visits the Studio

What beast must I adore? – Rimbaud

She said that we screwed once –
must have been drunk, she was so ugly
she was beautiful, her pogrom face,
its broad Ukrainian plains, sausage lips,

but legs that could kill a man,
a body that moved like oil on water,
sliding through the door
before I could kick her out.

★

The work was nothing much –
sub-Picasso – we were all doing
that kind of stuff. But Jack had
something, a gesture, a freedom,

I couldn't say, couldn't take my eyes
off his huge, broad hands, worker's
hands that could lay rails,
bend steel, break a girl in two.

Those big canvases
filled with the junk in his head,
loopy birds and twisted women.
I guess I fell in love.

★

She stood before *The Magic Mirror*
like it might swallow her whole,
her bird lips fluttering as if to speak,
small bird shoulders shaking,

she kept staring at my hands,
and I wanted to grab her, hit her,
kiss her, don't know what,
she had me so shook up,

she was like a cold jolt
of Russian vodka – straight.

★

The real deal, more of a man
than those Euro poseurs, with their
waxed-back hair, perfect
manners, smooth strokes.

He'll wrestle me to the floor
until I'm black and blue,
leave me wanting more, throw me
out the door. I'll keep coming back.

I said *you're sex on legs.*
Yes, he said, *I am.*

3. Springs

She taught herself to bake an apple pie
like a proper wife. She painted the kitchen
white – hallway, bedroom. Clean, bright,
new. He paced the rooms. She hid his booze.

She cooked his dinners, meat and potatoes the way
he liked, table set with a gingham cloth,
china plates, picked wildflowers to cheer
the vase, binned his gin. He threw a plate

against the wall, it smashed into a hundred
spiky scraps. Didn't want to be distracted
by the view, so he boarded up the windows
in the barn, locked the door. *No guests.*

Neighbours could hear them fighting a mile away,
both with mouths like sewers. She could give
as well as she could get. He called her *shrew.*
She threw another plate and spat

two can play at this. She banned his barroom
buddies, sent them packing back to the Cedar,
called his mother to whip him into shape.
A living hell, he said, and threw a plate,

threw the canvas on the ground and splashed
his paint. *A miracle,* he said, and raced
to show her. She gazed into his pool of rage,
Jack, that's a goddamn masterpiece.

4. Connected

I wanted people to sit still
for one goddamn minute but they
flash through your life –

        portraits are for the dead.

Trees construct themselves into a solid mass
as the horse picks up speed
see, everything's knotted
                together
the way notes on a staff spell music, a factory
churns out things, each thing
itself, but also a component.

How easy it is when density
unlaces, and you find holes you can
crawl through –
      light, a parting:

          Navajo bucks round
a campfire, dancing

if I half-close my eyes, I can make them
leap straight in.

5. Portrait of the Artist as a Depressed Bastard

His brow's a field of furrows,
his face half-cheek in shadow,
the night of the mind
descended, a silhouette of turmoil,
his cigarette mid-air.
Eyes too black, too deep,
and behind,
       the ghost mutt
tails him, the whistling
in his head, nature somewhere
in the distance, crusted,
tinged with sleep.
       And still he's coiled
in the cross and weave of giant screens:
casualties, market shares, Burger King.

6. Short Voyages

for Jackson and Frank

>   To digress
> is to be alive and know a mind
> at work, a body in motion,
> the blare of the city, in all its
> movements.
>   No accidents,
> only *cause* and *effect*, the future
> which is not so dark but which
> we cannot stop, speeding forward,
> destiny at the wheel.
>   Suddenly
> everything is lucid, shining,
> like children in the rain
> or a lover, naked, and they
> have to get it down,
>   witnesses
> to this age of flags and fear
> where art might have a place,
> sometimes right here on the street
> or in a bar
>   where men
> argue the world into being
> and drink to forget
> tomorrow we might be gone.

7. Rebel without a Cause

Lights. Camera. Action. Paint
whirls off the brush, as he drips
and dives:

GREATEST LIVING ARTIST IN AMERICA

Posing with his new Oldsmobile,
itching to take her out
for a spin, take in a matinee.

At the Regal lights dim
on the plush red, Jimmy's face
reels on the screen:

Once you been up there
you know you've been someplace.

The boy in Warnercolor, the boy
in the newsreel. Wheels
spun out, Porsche scrapped.
Like the magic trick, sawn in half.

The artist slumps in the row at the back.
He's seen this flick before:
I don't know what to do anymore.
Except maybe die.
                    Good trick:
exit stage right
before you crash and burn,
because tomorrow you'll be nothing.

Better to be a dead hero
than a deadbeat. Plush red,
lights dim.
            You can wake up now,
the universe has ended.

8. Cedar Nights

Kerouac baptised the ashtray with his piss,
Rothko gazed into his glass, lost
in a haze of smoke (later he would slit

each arm, two razored lines, maroon on white),
while Gorky picked a fight with every guy
who strayed within his reach (his wild eye,

hangdog face, peasant hands, the dreams
he couldn't shake). De Kooning pontificated
over water (bastard) and by his lead

women shattered into pieces, all lips
and tits. Klein splattered the bar in black,
while dizzy Ginsberg's angelheaded hipsters

swore, and sang, and toppled off their stools,
then hurled themselves into the negro streets;
Frank was brashly erecting something new

from shreds of Rauschenberg and Lady Day.
And Jack? He was painting up a storm
(when he was sober), admiring his fame

from the summit of the Gods, until the night
she breezed into the Cedar, all ass
and attitude, looking for a guy,

and there he was, the prize, the mark, the Jack
of Hearts, the cover boy. She sidled over:
what's a girl gotta do to get a drink?

9. Singing Woman

after Willem de Kooning

Her flame of notes
scorches the bar.
Stilettos, lips, nails
in Fire Engine, Hot Tamale, Cold Blood.

Naked under the strobe
that dissolves her dress,
fires her skin, brings her back

from the dead,
from the flat white
of an empty room, out cold, blood
oozing from her lip:

the kind of broad you want to hit.
Floozy. Hot Tamale.

Violence finds her
again and again, needle stuck,
a groove scratched by
Camels and coffee, a gin too many.

One way
down; the falling scale
lower, lower, as her angel
rises on a puff of smoke:

what you'd call
a torch song, tremulo of pain.

10. Death Car Girl

The nickname given to Pollock's lover, Ruth Kligman,
who survived the car crash that killed him

I pulled myself up from the forest mattress,
one of those wailing women
of Picasso's that you loved, my mascara,
black bars down my face, the neck of my dress
torn wide, like your animal rage.

But I was safe, alive – to walk again
through New York streets, accepting the eyes
of men in well-cut suits and ties, potential lovers
beneath their clothes. You watched them
watching me – your jealousy pierced my skin.

I walk into the Cedar where their stares
cling to me like flies; I hear their whispers
rise to a shout: *death car girl, death car girl,*
loud enough to raise you for one
last drink. And she,

furious widow, who would tear my hair
from its roots, smash my bones,
weighs on me like the granite boulder
on your grave. I want to tell her,
if she would hear me out,

how it was: I was your Monroe,
your moll, your late model cream puff,
woman enough to make you happy
(your old clown face bloated with misery),
your rush, your thrill, your speed.

11. Night Journey

Sleepless, she rises from their bed.

Wet grass soaks the hem of her nightdress,
a ghost in the moon's
weak glow.

In the barn, that strange aura,
like he's hiding somewhere,
playing tricks.
                His huge paintings
cower in the dark,
unfinished.

Night was always his time.
Now he's gone, she claims it:
             everything in black and white,
like newsprint.
                She can't deal with colours:
Yellow sun, too bright. Red knocks her out.
Blue, like death.

She's tired of dragging her body
from one place to another,
hearing the sound of her own voice,
waiting for nothing.

Only her brush is alive, moves blind
over the canvas, no longer eye
guiding hand.
            Stupid to think
he might be here. He'd hate to be
some dumb spirit, all air and solemnity.

If he were a ghost, she'd know.
He'd bring on a hurricane,
burn down the house.

This is her own spirit – breathing, finally
free. Her hand grabs black
from the sky, her feet
stick firm in the dirt.

12. Gothic Landscape

And still, this dream,
the one I've had for thirty years:
dark knot of trees, pulling myself through
undergrowth, my arms and legs
slashed by thorns. Black like nothing
I've ever known

not even your knitted
blacks, paint spooling on the canvas,
somewhere beneath, a body, a face; not even
your tortured nights, bottom of the bottle
and no peace; not even my empty nights,
feeling the tangle of our bodies
that first time when you whispered
do you like to fuck?

And now I'm old,
my taut girl's body replaced
by a maze of wrinkles and folds.
A gorgon, a harpie,
awaiting death.

Until death, this dream:
I'm crawling, my knees
cut and bleeding. Blind. But I have to keep
going, I know you are here, I know
I am too late – what I will find is the
wreckage of your body,
blood flooding the ground.

I wake, the bathroom mirror
horrified by my face, its gnarled surface
a witch's hollow,
a haunted forest.

13. Alchemy

Guggenheim, Venice

Just when I think nothing can move me,
room after room of Tintoretto, Veronese, Bellini,
the Virgin granting me her doleful eyes,
her pearly tears,

I enter a cool white palazzo,
find his huge canvas, which shows me the truth
of water and fire, in this place
of canals and candlelight, a city he never saw.

What he made was a world
in perpetual swirl, violent red, yellow bile,
the way the galaxy might look to a man stranded
in space, before science and logic takes hold.

And I stand before this picture,
the man who painted it
dead, like the masters shut away
in these palaces of art, their works their tribute;

wanting to pin beauty to the canvas,
dusty and flightless. But this picture lives, black
against the midday sun, legions of Day-Glo tourists
bobbing along the canal,

and I feel tears
welling up before I can make them stop.
I don't know why; I'm tired,
vulnerable in my light summer clothes,

he and I foreigners to a faith
which isn't ours: Christ on the cross,
the martyrdom of the saints, spelled out in
blood and gold.

from *Desire Paths* (2011)

We entered the city in autumn
the heat of summer still held in
the air, the map of our passions
ingrained in shaded boulevards
buildings solid like tombstones
& what I should not have done
I did not do, but sent a letter to
you to say I did (how to wound
with words) I have the capacity
to cut through concrete & glass
to undo the fragile construction
that cradles us, intricate scaffold
on the verge of collapse. I let go

We entered the city in autumn
there was a gallows on this spot
the guide book said, the pull of
death magnetic & do you think
a street can radiate fear forever?
do you smell evil on the water?
We will leave as we arrived, on
the verge of a major renovation
but the workmen are on strike
cranes are stalled, babel towers
blot the horizon, you were just
waiting for a fall & it's unlikely
we'll ever have reason to return

We entered the city in autumn
to the snare drum of the parade
beating us back to a boulevard
of the past, cool in heavy shade
buildings hulking like the Alps
you wrote a letter to your lover
who lived here long ago to say
you heard rumour of her death
& wished her all your very best
every building had a river view
every taxi turned into a coracle
every willow hung like a noose
the coldness in me won't thaw

We entered the city in autumn
it rained for twenty-three days
your umbrella snapped in half
under the deluge we stayed
indoors listening to time beating
a tinpot roof. Gallows weather
you said, as the rivers brimmed
over, the sea defences gave way
& the ruling party all fled south
you called a jumped-up hearse
to transport us to the city limits
the water followed in our wake
don't look back I heard you say

We entered the city in autumn
the coldest since records began –
they announced it on the news
you had to buy a pair of gloves
the cold seeped into our hands
our words like speech bubbles
in a cartoon, floating before us
encased in breath & our smiles
cracked like concrete. You are
a totem & I am frost, so winter
docks in the small of my throat
like a gallows. You tug at death
like a little boy tugging a sleeve

We entered the city in autumn
to the crack & blare of a tannoy
a mass evacuation, but you said
what is chemical warfare when
we have each other? The night
was red with sirens, the strange
disembodied voice, monotony
of disaster, so calm when hope is
finished. You made me laugh
when you entered in your gas
mask as a giant cartoon fly,
you never failed to make me laugh
that's what I will carry with me

We entered the city in autumn
accosted by a man pleading for
change, in front of the halfway
house, semi-conscious. So it's
come to this, you said, the end of
the line. We checked into a
hotel, the only guests, 24-hour
news on a loop, the explosion
again & again but the dead stay
dead. Are you cold? you asked
dragging a blanket over my feet
while the medics pull the sheet
over the head of the young girl

We'll leave the city in autumn
the most beautiful time of year
along the river where the dead
are garlanded like fairy lights &
cranes are stalled above rubble
the glass like lace, a burnt-out
shell of a dwelling place where
people like us lived & breathed
the concrete totems of our city
collapsed like cartoon cut-outs
you say take only what you can
carry, just leave the rest behind
& your memory fends for itself

from *Formerly* (2012)

Capacity

Fat chance you'll ever break out of here,
this depository for great mistakes
you've made your home. Just enough room
for a bed and a stool, a cell of sorts,
for a man of thin means. Lean times.
But I'm a girl who's capable
and culpable, who knows the value
of a pound. You can't resist the give
of my carapace, my caterpillar lips,
my capacious thighs. I'll never sell you
short. You'll never let me down.
For the first time, you are full
to the very brim with the milk
of human kindness. Moo.

Doors

Rows and rows, either side of the street,
stretching ahead of her, like mirrors
in mirrors. Behind each, a different shade
of carpet; the fine dust of misery.
Some bells chime like Big Ben, others
play a little tune; she's never welcome,
with her scuffed shoes, her *Watchtower*,
The Good News That No One Will Hear.
There was a man once, well-dressed;
he stood on her threshold, always coming
or going. It didn't matter either way.
She keeps a key to a lock that won't fit,
a house no longer standing. *The door
is always open* he said, leaving.

Flat Iron Square

No *you are here* to show you where:
ass-end of nowhere, you are square
off the map, circling your steps
like a dog tracking a trail of piss.
A curse, a rasp, a chokedamp cough,
a stifled laugh. Their faces graze
the faded smiles of plywood – little kids
with thumbs for eyes, skin clingfilmed
over bones, mouths wide as caves:
you look as if you've seen a ghost.
What a waste, your lousy life, your
flat-iron face. The corners curling
with boredom. Now you're one of them,
a stooge in the room, a stench.

Inch & Co Cash Chemists

The stench of hash met his nose,
cocaine-catch in his chest. He hitched
the hem of his moth-ash coat, stashed
the mess – a case of cats & mice.

A mash on the chin, a stitch – a Scotch
to thin the ache. Once he tossed a coin –
China or Cheam; an itch in the mists
of time. He missed the hit, the scent

of sin, the chime of cents. Same shit –
the *can't* of cant, the stain of shame.
The months aim mace at him. That's it,
in the can. Do the maths – he's mince.

Me, I'm chaste, I'm sane.
I am his chain, his match.

X-Zalia Night Cure

For cuts, wounds, bruises, scratches,
burns or scalds, eczema, rashes,
any break or wound in the skin,
diseases caused by insects, vermin;
catarrh, rose cold, colds in the head,
influenza, poisoned blood,
piles, fistulas, leucorrhœa,
hives, shingles, diarrhœa.
Ideal injected, or as a spray,
douche or lotion, once a day,
to the mouth, throat, nose, ear,
vagina, uterus, bladder, urethra.
Follow instructions on the label:
just one dose to heal what ails you.

Duk   of   gton

Gone, the days of ho fun duck,
back of the truck fooling around,
white guy funk, goon squad drunks,
a ton of laughs. I nearly puked.
Forgotten in the glummy dusk,
a glutton for a punch up. Fuck it.
I'm done with doom, dark core
of nothing, morning lost, the *ack ack*
of a crow on a branch, same old, same old.
Don't even know what's
missing, though there's a hole
in my heart, an ache in my brain,
a pandora's trunk of trouble,
and no one to open me up.

Quickie Heel Bar

Ladies, here's the shit:
your skirt's so tight you can barely walk,
your stillies *clack clack* like a ticking clock.
You strut to the bar for a rum and coke,
scan the joint for a bloke with a wad,
some blow to share, a flair for words:
I'm your Cyrano without the hooter,
your Romeo with a better future,
your Casanova with a Rolodex,
your Ronaldo with Italian treads.
I can go all night like the Duracell Bunny,
not being funny. I'm a bull in the ring,
I'll make you *ring a ding ding*, no bull.
Ladies, get your coats, you've pulled.

Limehouse Cut

You slumped into the night. That was it:
I fling myself at exits, breezeblock walls,
I haunt abandoned lots, urinal stalls,
anywhere that bears your mark (the flick
of the switch and then the dark, the quickie fuck),
any place you had me, any way;
like they said you'd do, you chucked me away
like trash; like shit on your shoe, I'm stuck
in the past; I'm pissed. Now I splash my tears
over the ragged towpath of your estate
and wait for rain to wash the morning clear,
and wait for love to incubate from hate,
and wait for spring to strip the sky of soot,
and wait for pain to crack your concrete heart.

The Rose

Your memory's turning tricks; a sudden
blush as you relive the bump and grind,
the slap and tickle. It was all a giggle,
didn't care about the consequences, cold
light of day, and all of that: a dab of
La Vie En Rose behind the ear, a skinful,
and you were set. *No regrets*, that's what
she sang, *no regrets*, but you forget
what it was like when you could clench
the thorny branch between your teeth,
dance all night for the boys. Your heart's
playing tricks; the stop / start / stop,
that voice, clear as a bell in your mind:
Hurry up, gentlemen, please, it's time.

Iron Urns

A park, *rus in urbe*, a place to rest
in peace, with roses, weeping willow:

but we can't contain the dead,
they're roused from sleep to sour the air,
rusting every crack and crevice, a breath
that smuts the back of necks; they're reduced
to ash, the lug of bone made light
as laughter shivering the trees.

We bear the weight of stones and slabs,
heaving marble garlands, plaques proclaiming
great works and deeds. They can't release
their grip, their names chiselled
into benches where we sit. They thrust
themselves upon us, insist we don't forget.

Sacred to the memory

Not even stone can hold us, words
erased in poison air. We speak without words,
with our eyes, our works, and etch
our shapes in memory; frail lace etched
in the brain. In poison air we speak
with angels, scrolls and glyphs. We speak
in memory, its frail lace, honour
what has turned to dust; we honour
stone. Even stone will turn to dust
where all around us is erased, and dust
remembers nothing, no eyes, no shapes.
We hold on to words: how we shaped
our lives, our works (they vanish into air),
how we etched *memory* in the air.

Whitechapel

The trees imprison me, rigid wardens.
I match them in my stillness, my stiff
resolve. The marrow of the dead
seeps into their roots, they carry omens
in their leaves. I cannot leave

as long as they are watching.
They smuggle night inside their trunks
and in daylight, crowd the glass with shadows.
They reflect their frozen sky in me,
my sightless eye, my hardened cheek.

The bars caress my face, a grid of days.
The world is square, like the map
that shows us where we are: I am here.
You are somewhere else.

Final Clearance

Fin, Fine, End, that's all.
It's clear that once upon a time
you were the life and soul,
the duke of blue o'clock.
You clamp your ear to the keyless hole,
hear the gasp of the airless room,
stroke the hopeless chipboard;
you'll never mend the broken pane.

You're the final straw, a fatal flaw,
a cul-de-sac (you can't turn back),
a double fault, the family vault,
the worked-out mine, the battle line,
the prison camp, the rising damp,
a parting sigh . . . the long goodbye.

Formerly

This depository for great mistakes
stretches ahead of us, like mirrors
in mirrors. What a waste. The ass-end
of nowhere, square off the map, circling
our steps. A Scotch would thin the ache,
heal what ails us; dark core of nothing,
don't even know what's missing.
But here's the shit: we're stuck in the past,
memory's turning tricks. That voice,
clear as a bell in our minds, insists
we don't forget. We honour
dust; trees smuggle night inside
this airless room. I hear your breath,
its rising fall, its long *goodbye*.

New Poems

Carmen

The mirror fairgrounds her face:
clown with a rosy gob.

She's a single glove in the snow
frozen porcelain hard.

She's made of lace and stone,
sports a posy pressed to pulp.

She swings him close to her heart,
he's her ball and chain;

his face is black and white
shut tight in a cage of gold.

She wears a balcony bra,
takes the orchestra for a spin.

Only a matter of time
until the stiletto in the spine,

the fanfare of farewell:
she makes her bed.

Lace

I drape myself in lace,
pretty trappings of the widow,
that hide a tangled mass
of arteries and veins – a mess of pain.

My face, a mask of skin:
peel it back to find the frame of bone,
deep holes that hold my eyes,
Marvelous Wondergraphs of the soul.

The craze of age, a trail across
the brow's terrain, it's plain
what I try to stem in vain
will get me in the end:

the wrinkle in the plan,
a tinny little laugh that lodges
in the gullet, the lop of blood
stopped in its tracks,

the cack hand of death,
clammy, yes, like in the movie,
moving swiftly through me,
capillaries of black.

Swimmer of Lethe

after Tom de Freston

A momentary parting before
water recovers water,

and water doesn't remember
the blunt impression,

the heroic effort, it's flat
and heartless. No mirror,

no hippy-dip calm, but sharp
and dark, metallic.

I think I could get to like it,
relinquish

the vertical world: buildings,
trees, my standing self;

I've mastered surface,
here everything is *under.*

The deathy drink
sweetens my mouth,

floods my veins, my blood
cleansed clear,

I will go white like marble.

Snow Globe

From his distant clime he rules the weather,
conjures blizzards with the flick of his wrist;
a thrillion crystals prick my skin,
quiver me in white. I am his Winter
Queen, resident of the silvery palace,
I sleep on a bed of ice. I wear a gown
glazed with stalactites that shatter as I dance,
my glass slippers ermined in snow.
I'm his slip-of-a-girl, shrink-to-size squeeze,
but with a wave he could command an early thaw,
release me from this perishing freeze;
he's a bitter king who swears by his own law
so I am slave to his inclement heart
that pumps chill blood, knows no heat.

The Little Ice Age

The freeze that put trees to sleep
shrouded steeples, cast drunkards
who fell short of their beds
in marble effigies. A quicksilver city
crowned the solid river, mansions
without foundations.

The frost made merry sport:
skaters coupled with their reflections,
children and dogs yelped with glee
at their foolish legs. The people were dazzled,
each step lively and dangerous.

Some heard the low rumble
trebling to a cry, saw the shatter webbing
the surface, and, before the man could flee,
the surge of break widened at his feet,
pulling him under the icy sheet,

but most did not, content to live
in the suspension between freeze
and thaw, easy in their play. No one
wished for spring, with its sentimental
blooms and twittering birds;
the strange and fatal fevers
carried on the first warm breeze.

Floor

I walk your surface, over nicks and scars.
I want to finish. I find my image in your varnish.
My bones are weary pearls.

I fell hard for your pack of lies, your pearls
of wisdom; when in truth you scar
foundations, hold the faces of the vanished

in your face. Their eyes are varnished,
they come to me in dreams, like salvaged pearls.
You undermine me, you are never scared;

your pearly words will scar then vanish.

Construction

For months it has risen, invading my window,
boxing the sky in steel. Most days I neglect to see it,
focused on interiors, the screen of words,
but the grey box shouts; concrete and metal
submitting to the hydraulic, the cry of the saw
splitting air.

            When the wrecking ball
opens another new vista we forget the silhouette
of walls removed; we ignore blocks condemned, shuddering
in their foundations, squatters' flags still draped,
curtains for high ideals.

                  The empty plot forgets
clothes strewn on vanished floors, spoons and frying pans;
in demolition the goal is ground,
we are out in the open.

                  We coat ourselves in steel
but the blast always shakes us, the delicate bell
of breaking glass. The column topples,
dissolving into its components, a pile of ash.
Minutes to trash, months to erect, years
to understand how to occupy – each on top of the other,
our stacked-up lives.

Legend

That place – lost to you now,
just coordinates on a map (the map
you carried in your pocket), a grey wedge
for parkland: sudden spike of cut grass

and there's the oak in your sights, branches
laced with lichen, its canopy of leaves
towering the parched field, crazy paving
of ants marching in its shade, trunk furrowed.
You say the name aloud, the place you lost
reduced to a word, rough bark on your tongue.

Years go by. Towns vanish in the creases,
rubbed clean to white; you can't recall their names.
It remains, each branch precise in your mind,
the oak, still green in the dead of winter.

A View from the Ness, towards the Village of Orford

The Old Masters would not have imagined this:
our century's junk – components of surveillance
strewn on the ground, metal wind-twisted,
blushed with rust; machines that powered our lives
battered and crushed.
                    The rest they'd understand:
clouds hoarding dull pewter, path curving
to greet the bridge; the village on the horizon,
peaks of church and castle – god and guns ready
for the invasion that never came.
                          Now it's always
winter – tall grass in umber, burnt sienna, the land
shutting down. A single figure strides forward
along the flat expanse of shingle, the place
where all things shed their past.

The Muntjac

reflects our headlights in his eyes;
his scrubby body disappears into the hedge

now white with May,
tar and fern on his delicate hooves

and all at once the road reverts
to emptiness, but something of his presence

stays, an apparition on the verge:
fugitive from walled estates that favoured

curiosities, alien tropics *quick and rank*,
snaking beyond the boundaries, laying roots.

The road curves past Darks Dale floodlit,
a tractor ploughing furrows, past New Broke Ups,

Wrong Land; and beyond, a tangle of forest,
oaks hunched like old men against the night.

Other Landscapes

He is the only passenger in coach A. The light is cold and casts everything in green; it hurts his eyes. He searches for a view from the window but receives only his reflection, twice. Scattered lights break the black. He is beyond the city, somewhere in Essex. Occasionally, the train shudders through a local station without slowing, the name swept away in the urgency of movement. He thinks of that poem, the unwonted station, the name he can't remember. He wants the journey to be over, to be lying in his bed, but he is heading in the opposite direction from home. He will stay in a commuter hotel next to the airport, where the thrum of planes taking off will disrupt his sleep. He will dream of great engines firing in the night, the bulk of a factory, hunched figures without faces.

He remembers a long car journey, linger of stale cigar in the back seat, how he felt sick. He played games with the cars, counting all the blue ones, then the white ones, then finding Qs in the number plates, until he was bored by games. He can't remember much, a visit to distant family not seen since, but he can still picture the back of his mother's head, her brown hair piled high, tied with a white ribbon. She didn't move or speak for the entire journey. His father kept trying to tune the radio, but the programme faded in and out, another voice insistent, loud, and he thought of the sound of them arguing behind their bedroom door, how he could never hear his mother, her voice hardly raised beyond a whisper, just his father's dominant baritone: *over my dead body*.

He gets lost on the way to the church. The satnav directs him to St Christopher's Road, but the church is another mile, a 70s breeze-block structure chosen for its proximity to the funeral home. When he finally arrives, he will push open the heavy door and squint at the interior gloom. His brother will glare and tap his watch before they take their places at the front. The vicar, who didn't know him, will speak of his father as a good man. On the way out, strangers will come up and offer condolences. But before he goes in, he is halted by a tree over the road, a magnolia, brightening a concrete wall, white petals tinged with pink. In another week, it will shed its blossom – but now, at the moment he has stopped to look, despite being late, it is in full bloom.

He watches the mechanical construction of time, digital numbers flaring red: 7 fattening to 8, diminishing to 9. At 04:11 he switches on the bedside light. A room service menu slides onto the floor with a thud. His eyes can't adjust. Someone is snoring in 504, loud, long inhalations. The dream has left his mouth furred and dry; he can't remember it fully – he should have waited in the dark for the images to fix. There was a beach, a place he thought he knew, beyond a low wall constructed in the sand ridge, a defence erected during the war. He is walking towards a gap in the brick, but each step becomes more difficult than the last, his feet catch in the sand and sink. He can hear the waves breaking on the shore, children laughing. He wakes before he can reach the sea.

He turns the OS map so the sea is behind him, but the field he stands in doesn't seem to exist. He smoothes the crease, in case it's hiding in the fold, turns it again. He looks up to identify landmarks: the field slopes to the north, to a line of poplars leaning in the wind. It is a field without characteristics. The wind picks up and grabs a corner of the map, folding it in on itself. He walks to the northeast corner, finds a stile, a trace of footpath running parallel to the fence. The sheep look up from their grazing and stare. He can make out a ruined structure on the far hill, a farmhouse perhaps, a refuge for the shepherd. The roof has gone, but the walls are still intact; through one he can see a square of sky. On the map he locates the word *ruin*. It begins to rain.

He finds her picture on the internet. She hasn't changed. He can't tell if she's married; these days women keep their names. No personal information, just a small number of entries to do with work, a conference she organised, a company email. He thinks about sending a message, decides against it. They had a holiday once in Spain; there was a dusty road leading to a derelict church, the salt flats beyond, white residue on his boots for weeks after they returned, even after they finished. He was too hot to keep walking, but she wanted to see inside the church. The road stretched straight ahead, the church never any closer. But she was determined, a few paces in front, her hair pale in the sun, her shoulders burned. He closed his eyes and saw her dark outline, the trace of her.

He is stuck in traffic. The driver in front keeps leaning on his horn, as if his frustration might propel him forward. He opens the window but even the air isn't moving. A bus pulls alongside, its passengers occupied by newspapers and tablets. As the bus slowly moves forward, it reveals two men at the kerb digging into a dirt square in the pavement slabs. One of the men brings out a spiky palm from the back of a wheeled cart – the kind you might normally see in tropical climates. Along its razored green edges are bright streaks of red. They lower it into the hole they've dug, patting the dirt in place. The pavement is altered by its presence, a strange alien, and he thinks maybe he's never really been at home anywhere. The light changes; the driver behind leans on his horn.

He realises he has left his camera back at the hotel. The bus bumps along an unmade road, the guide pointing out various sites, his fellow tourists holding their lenses against the smudged window. Ruined temples dot the landscape, columns spiking the horizon. Just a pile of stones, his father would have said, so what? The air conditioning is broken; it wheezes like an old man trying to breathe, it's difficult to make out what the guide is saying. Something about Zeus. He looks through the window at the parched ground. This ancient place, this history, so what? He has become his father. He wonders when it was he lost his curiosity. These days, he can only take in so many new things. The guide says something about Aphrodite. He sits in his seat, stares straight ahead.

Ruin

The guidebook talks of famine and war;
the field is peaceful enough: a few cows
stare and chew and stare.

The heroic fort brought down
by tare. Where there was a door, now
a black gasp. The wind shrieks, spikes grass.

Fear keeps this place alive with its stink.
Granite is patient, weathers
death, wears the sheen of storm, stands

with the same grey demeanour
day and night, to remind us of our failure,
where we went wrong.

              talks of   war;
      field   peaceful
stare   and stare.

      heroic
                        a door, now
      black

      keeps this place alive
              patient
                        storm, stands

          same grey
day and night,   our failure,
where we went wrong.

              talks of
        peace

      hero
                        or, no
      black

                        storm

          night   o   failure,
      here we went wrong.

Isle of Grain

Even the name's not right:
not *grain* but *greon*, gravel
under a slab sky,

not even an island, a spit;
to the east the river's mouth
opens to feed the sea.

Dark wound of a pillbox
defends nothing, no one left,
apart from kids who mark

the tarmac with glyphs, a giant
GPS, a real laugh. Now birds
rule – the marsh underworld

hums with life, if you know
how to search. Rush sprouts
from concrete, resilient.

Last stand. The wind calls, keeps
calling. There's nowhere
to go but away.

AL 151

condenses distance, snubs the land;
no one cares, on their way to
somewhere else – there must be

somewhere else. Here's where
boredom sleeps; it breeds
in the heat, dreams of shade.

Along the *autovía* parched *stipa*
clings to rock, barbed wire
snakes the ground:

no reason for trespass, nothing
to protect. The definition
of nowhere. A low building lies

deserted, a place of industry
failed, and beyond, *las colinas*
hoarding the sun – the sun

just over the next ridge
so we must keep going,
dead set.

After the Storm

At daybreak cars crept along the main road
out of town, luggage racks piled
with huddled bundles.

Those of us who stayed
stockpiled batteries, bottled water, canned beans.

The streets emptied of everything but heat.
A couple of storm chasers
cruised in like they owned the place;
one of them would die years later in Texas,
the tornado whisking him off the ground like a leaf.

When it finally arrived, its black hand tore
through whole fields, tossed aside houses and trees,
grabbed the sun in its fist.

I always believed each morning
I'd wake, each day would bring
some new joy.
           I survived
but now fear squats in my heart
ready to fling me to the sky.

Sinister Little Flower

your leper bell tolls the first
gong of spring; you leapfrog the stile,
sprinkling poison petals in your fall,
scattering your bloody drops

like a consumptive. And in your thrall
we slink along your snaky dirge
as we sneak along the verge
like villains, your velvety pall

pulling us in, the shade of sin
lush in the languid air.
Deadly ladies, we are ensnared
by your beautiful bruise, your pain.

Knotweed

Durable, your rough roots, your troops;
your line of destruction

that moles its way beneath foundations –
it will outlive us.

We are coming and going, always lost and losing,
in love with the tug of leaving, the future

cast upon the shaded map, the Alice Universe
expanding:

all roads are chosen, all roads say *come*;
your greedy paws claw all for one

to feed your lust for land,
you grab the lot.

Fleeceflower, the fleet hour of inflorescence
bursts, you drape your skirts

over the earth, tough peduncle,
homunculus. You will not budge

now you've found your calling: the felling
of our failing structures.

Yarn

i.m. Fred Sandback, 1943–2003

Everything's strung together, little bits of matter.
You gather old haunts, taunting songs, random loops of time:
cat's cradle caught between your fingers. You don't linger;
turn it out and start again.

I know in my veins I've been here before; the field more
music than static, magnetic force between two things.
It's not long – this hollow, this place, our movement through space:
string me along, I'll follow.

The tales I spin are wearing thin – unlace this noose, un-
loose the mass of solid constructs, mess of life and limb.
What's outside isn't in, what's inside is hard to out:
I have learned to live with doubt.

You leave a tangled web; we interweave, then untie
the knot. Your cord is taut, and long enough to hang my
knit and purl of words. Another yarn – nothing new, but
something more: an opened door.

Gatekeeper

I am your port of entry, the point of no return,
you yield to my kludgy touch,
the Magic Fingers you can't switch off. I am a screen

for your sins, discreet, like a Venetian blind you shut
to kill the light. I am night,
starless, sharp with little cries; you navigate through touch.

I am the goddess Kali of a thousand fingers,
I'll stroke, stroke until a scream
rises from your gut, the beast unfurled, a masterpiece

of hurt. I am your Painted Lady, your Queen of Spain,
a wing in the rake of thorns;
I cling to you like grave clothes, the suit you'll never shake.

I am the circus freak, the double act of one. Gone
through a gash, flash in the pan;
it doesn't last, the searing lash of pain, slash of skin,

peek-a-boo of blood. I'm in the driver's seat, the scent
of burning flesh, gasoline
quivering my nostrils; I'm full-throttle towards the wall.

I am the swallow in your throat, hollow in your heart,
deep rut of the furrowed field.
I slay without a sound, here inside my velvet box.

Wing Mirror

The ravine is a tangle of thorns, hubcaps, all the jagged edges of the night; kids scare each other shitless, drink and fuck until the blue light ghosts the trees. The ravine is a scar, a wound that opens wide, close to the burial sites of Escorts laced with rust; wing mirrors, eyes that never shut. Secrets stuck in the mud rise to the surface in rain: the fire extinguished, the party finished. Time to leave.

The ravine is a scar, a wound, a jagged secret. Kids party, drink fire, fuck in the mud; rust like shit sticks to the surface of hubcaps. Ghosts escort them to the edge of the burial site, mirror the night: blue light extinguished in rain. They rise on tangled wings laced with thorns, their eyes are shut. The ravine is open wide, never scared. The trees close their leaves.

The ravine is shit, a fucking thorn in the eye. Kids wing it, tangled up and blue. They drink until their secrets are buried, score surface wounds on hubcaps, scare the ghosts wide from the trees. They fire open night, the party never shuts. In the rain and mud they lace their scars with rust. They rise and leave before their time is finished. Extinguished. The mirror's jagged edge sticks them in its sights. The ravine closes the light.

The ravine is edged with a light surface of rain. Mirrors rust; the fire extinguished like a ghost. Shitty site to be buried: stuck in the drink, in the mud, like a hubcap. Don't tangle with the night; time is a party that finishes in a ravine; out of the blue your escort's fucked off, and you're a thorn in a wing. Don't be scared, kids. Never rise to the secret that shuts the eyes. Wounds close, but they leave scars.

Pictures of Spring

1. Shunga

The geisha parts her legs
to receive his cock,
a monstrous cryptid, swollen fist;

I cannot see her face
behind the fragile net, a strand
of hair fallen from its comb

but her sex is open wide,
complex, a darkened gorge
he will wreck.

2. Tōkyo Metro / Ginza Line

The businessman next to me
balances a briefcase on his knees,
opens his *manga*:

two doe-eyed girls in gym slips,
hair in bunches, are ripped apart
by tigers.

The artist has taken pride
in the tearing of limbs,
the beauty of the tiger.

3. Isetan Department Store, Shinjuku

The girl behind the counter
converts a sheet of paper
into a full blown rose:

she works quickly, her fingers
light, thin, her hair falls
across her face;

as she hands me this gift
without looking up, she nods,
a blush masking her cheeks.

4. Ukiyo

I bend and break, bend
and break, contort my limbs
into these lovelocked shapes,

my desires spread out
like the fingered leaves
of a pillow book;

I resume the polite tedium
of clothes, desire folded in on itself –
a sharp intake of breath

Insomnia

The clock's small hands carry me
to the house where I was a child

and in those rooms peace settled
despite the war inside the TV,
the lunatic with an axe who filled
the drive-in screen. My parents said
no harm would come if I was good.

My room was buttercup yellow,
it was always spring; my Barbies
were missing arms or legs, while boys
came back from Nam in bags.
Everyone seemed old but they were young,

now everyone seems young, and I'm the one
crowding the night with phantoms.

Hospital time

collapses, folds the days into sterile gauze,
            a thousand different words for hurt.

The body breaks and bruises and still it ticks,
a tarnished watch. Never the right time.
Never enough.

The one-legged smokers at the entrance
stoke the furnace of their disappearance,

the woman in the crowded lift
cries into her hands,

                 and the man who's a dead ringer
for the elderly Liszt bangs out Brahms
on an out-of-tune piano
while the nurses eat crisps and gaze into their phones.

Outside, the majestic bridge,
the pompous clock,
the tourists and buses

and somewhere tucked away in these corridors, my mother
hooked up to her whistles and bells,

the frail lines that keep her alive;
older by centuries, exhausted.

Her little bag of blood, not red,
more rust, like the dirty river
through the window.

Never
      enough.

Clear Water

She must have been his daughter, the woman
visiting the man in the bed next to my mother,

our lives rubbing together in the glare of the HDU,
a thin curtain between us. She'd brought him

a book of poems by Seamus Heaney, *you like him,
don't you?* And then she filled the ward with words;

Anahorish, my place of clear water, and the ward
opened, as her mouth opened and sounded his words,

which could smooth the steel and bleep of monitors.
The nurses did not hear, they had learned to block

the small talk of families who know they need to keep
talking, and poems are not expected, have no place;

the language of the ward is the condition of change,
never the world outside the ward, never the place

where we began to see the world differently, where
mound-dwellers go waist-deep in mist to break

the light ice. The ice had melted in my mother's glass,
she was sleeping when the words entered the ward,

she did not hear. And the next day, she was dead,
and a few months later, the poet too was dead,

and I keep wondering about the woman and her
father, and if he made it, if he is still breathing.

Skull

A middle-aged man, black jeans, spiky hair,
black tee: a skull emblazoned on his chest –
symbol of Black Sabbath, or Napalm Death,
one of those metal bands that wears the reaper

lightly – at odds with daffs and furry kittens
around intensive care, where he now sits
while the skull on his chest winks and grins;
and I think of Masaccio's crucifixion,

how Christ has died in agony and the Marys
gather to pray at the cross's base for glorious
resurrection; below, a skeleton lies
in state: *as I am now so will you be,*

the way the man he visits, maybe his father,
lies, frail amid the sheets. Judgement
comes to him in the guise of the terrible head,
if he is able to open his eyes. Fear

suspends the ward, the word we cannot speak,
but this man sports death on his chest like God
and I want to shake him, say: there is no God,
there is no faith, and what you do is mock

the vigil we are forced to make together,
what scrap of dignity we still possess –
all of us here simply watching, powerless
to change the end. I sit beside my mother,

charting her final breaths, and when, without
any warning, they just cease, I see
how she departed from her body, leaving
a hollow case, all the life pulled out.

A Letter to WS Graham

Sydney – if I may call you Sydney – because I feel
you have been speaking to me all this time,
in the complex, common tongue you attempted
to decipher. And I've been listening, here
by the sea you said was listening. It is a space,
the sea, like all the other spaces you tried to
(de)construct, it is a poem that finds its turn
along the shoreline; a lament, a plain-
tive voice, like the mother of a drowned child.

The light is variable, and I write to hold it against
the shadows. It's all we can ever do – try to hold
a moment disappearing even as we whisper its name
and place it in the light. Break here, stop
your difficult glances and cantankerous rambles.
Tell me
            how to say something about the sea that
hasn't been said in thousands of words, stumbling
across the page like drunks, none of them up to the
job. The job is love, you said,
that's why we stretch ourselves into a thousand
suffering shapes, like Hilton's nudes or Lanyon's thermals.
You made words of their colours, made words
for the sea that fancies itself a metaphor, too pretty
and brutal for simple truth.
                        Tell me
now that your words are done, how to keep going on.
The coast stretches too far for me to see,
but you're ahead, in a lonely place (we make our own,
you said); from there you must be able to see us all,
lighting lamps with our voices.

You are the lighthouse now, beaming
and winking, gently guiding us away
from the treacherous rocks.

To Crysse
with love + admiration.
So good to see you!
        T x

184

The Formula for Night

It's getting late. Light
floods the public bar,
you're the final one to leave.
The mirror's silver eye
gives you back yourself, precise.
You've lived your life through
glass, you miss the brush

of skin, someone whispering
your name. You hear it now,
a calling on the wind, insistent,
a small but steady flame.
You carry in your bones a gasp
of summer heat, the formula
for night. You arrive at the end-

of-pier reveal – the heart-stop hour,
when this world briefly yields
to the next: a door that creaks
an inch or two to catch
a blinding beam. You want
to understand what can't
be seen, the fact behind

the trick, the wires hidden
from your view, the blue breath
that powers the machine.
Raise your eyes to read the stars –
streetlight's glare has cast them
dark; once-bright bulbs,
trembling elements crack

and fizzle as they die. Their light
is obsolete. But close
your eyes, and still you find
gold impressed beneath
your lids, a moment lived.
And when you open them again,
darkness is what's left.

Acknowledgements

This book includes poems from the following collections: *Sweetheart* (Slow Dancer Press, 1998), *Barnard's Star* (Enitharmon, 2004), *Fetch* (Salt, 2007) and *The City with Horns* (Salt, 2011). It also includes poems from three collaborative artists' books: *Marks* (with Linda Karshan, printed and published by Pratt Contemporary, 2007), *Desire Paths* (with Linda Karshan, Galerie Hein Elferink, 2012) and *Formerly* (with Vici MacDonald, Hercules Editions, 2012). I would like to thank Linda Karshan, Bernard and Susan Pratt, Hein Elferink and Vici MacDonald for granting permission to include images from those earlier publications in this book, and also to the Redfern Gallery, especially Richard Selby, for their support of my collaboration with Linda.

Acknowledgements are due to the following anthologies and print and online magazines who have published more recent poems: *By the North Sea: An Anthology of Suffolk Poetry* (Shearsman, 2013), *Poetry London, Shearsman* magazine, *Ambit, The Rialto, Interlitq, Long Poem Magazine, Magma, Poetry Wales, The SHOp, Writers' Hub* and *The Stare's Nest*.

'Floor' was commissioned by *Magma* for the 50th Issue Poetry Competition Prize Event in 2012. 'A Letter to WS Graham' was written during a residency at Caroline Wiseman's Aldeburgh Beach South Lookout Tower in 2013. 'Construction' was commissioned for the Magdalene College Festival of Sound in 2015 and formed a collaboration with the sound artist Douglas Benford.

A number of poems were written in response to exhibitions and the work of particular artists: the title poem was commissioned by the Southbank Centre for *Light Show* at the Hayward Gallery (2013) and is based on an installation by Cerith Wyn Evans (my thanks to White Cube for granting permission to use the cover image); 'Forest' was commissioned by Ekphrasis for *Sensing Spaces* at the Royal Academy (2014); 'Lace', 'Knotweed', 'Gatekeeper' and 'Wing Mirror' were written for the artist Alison Gill on the occasion of her exhibition *Legend Trip* at the Charlie Dutton Gallery (2012); 'Swimmer of Lethe' was commissioned by Tom de Freston for the anthology *The Charnel House* (Bridgedoor Press, 2014) and is based on his painting of the same title.

My special thanks to the artist David Harker, who invited me to write a sequence informed by his exhibition *Species of Trees and Other Landscapes* at the Islington Arts Factory in 2014. The poems 'AL 151', 'Other Landscapes', 'Isle of Grain' and 'Ruin' are inspired by his work and were published originally in the collaborative edition *Nowheres* (2015).

My thanks also to Mick Felton, Amy Wack and Jamie Hill at Seren, and to friends and poets who have given invaluable advice on recent poems: Anne Berkeley, Claire Crowther, Tim Dooley, Annie Freud, Roddy Lumsden, Rhona McAdam, Sue Rose, Robert Stein, Siriol Troup and the members of Colin Falck's workshop. I would also like to thank those who have given support and encouragement over the twenty years that span the writing of the poems in this collection, especially Martyn Crucefix, Sheenagh Pugh and Andrew Lindesay.

Well chosen words

Seren is an independent publisher with a wide-ranging list which includes poetry, fiction, biography, art, translation, criticism and history. Many of our books and authors have been on longlists and shortlists for – or won – major literary prizes, among them the Costa Award, the Jerwood Fiction Uncovered Prize, the Man Booker, the Desmond Elliott Prize, The Writers' Guild Award, Forward Prize and TS Eliot Prize.

At the heart of our list is a beautiful poem, a good story told well or an idea or history presented interestingly or provocatively. We're international in authorship and readership though our roots are here in Wales (Seren means Star in Welsh), where we prove that writers from a small country with an intricate culture have a worldwide relevance.

Our aim is to publish work of the highest literary and artistic merit that also succeeds commercially in a competitive, fast changing environment. You can help us achieve this goal by reading more of our books – available from all good bookshops and increasingly as e-books. You can also buy them at 20% discount from our website, and get monthly updates about forthcoming titles, readings, launches and other news about Seren and the authors we publish.

www.serenbooks.com